Multicultural America

Volume II
The Arab Americans

Multicultural America

Volume II

The Arab Americans

Rodney P. Carlisle
GENERAL EDITOR

Facts On File
An imprint of Infobase Publishing

Multicultural America: Volume II: The Arab Americans
Copyright © 2011 by Infobase Publishing

Facts On File, Inc.
An Imprint of Infobase Publishing
132 West 31st Street
New York, NY 10001

Library of Congress Cataloging-in-Publication Data
Multicultural America / Rodney P. Carlisle, general editor.
    v. cm.
    Includes bibliographical references and index.
    Contents: v. 1. The Hispanic Americans — v. 2. The Arab Americans — v. 3. The African Americans — v. 4. The Asian Americans — v. 5. The Jewish Americans — v. 6. The European Americans — v. 7. The Native Americans.
    ISBN 978-0-8160-7811-0 (v. 1 : hardcover : alk. paper) — ISBN 978-0-8160-7812-7 (v. 2 : hardcover : alk. paper) — ISBN 978-0-8160-7813-4 (v. 3 : hardcover : alk. paper) — ISBN 978-0-8160-7814-1 (v. 4 : hardcover : alk. paper) — ISBN 978-0-8160-7815-8 (v. 5 : hardcover : alk. paper) — ISBN 978-0-8160-7816-5 (v. 6 : hardcover : alk. paper) — ISBN 978-0-8160-7817-2 (v. 7 : hardcover : alk. paper) 1. Minorities—United States—History—Juvenile literature. 2. Ethnology—United States—History—Juvenile literature. 3. Cultural pluralism—United States—History—Juvenile literature. 4. United States—Ethnic relations—Juvenile literature. I. Carlisle, Rodney P.
    E184.A1M814 2011
    305.800973—dc22   2010012694

3|12

Facts On File books are available at special discounts when purchased in bulk quantities for businesses, associations, institutions, or sales promotions. Please call our Special Sales Department at (212) 967-8800 or (800) 322-8755.

You can find Facts On File on the World Wide Web at http://www.factsonfile.com

Text design and composition by Golson Media
Cover printed by Art Print, Taylor, PA
Book printed and bound by Maple Press, York, PA
Date Printed: March 2011
Printed in the United States of America

11 10 9 8 7 6 5 4 3 2 1

This book is printed on acid-free paper.

CONTENTS

Volume II

The Arab Americans

AMERICANS HAVE HAD a sense that they were a unique people, even before the American Revolution. In the 18th century, the settlers in the thirteen colonies that became the United States of America began to call themselves Americans, recognizing that they were not simply British colonists living in North America. In addition to the English, other cultures and peoples had already begun to contribute to the rich tapestry that would become the American people.

Swedes and Finns in the Delaware River valley, Dutch in New York, Scots-Irish, and Welsh had all brought their different ways of life, dress, diet, housing, and religions, adding them to the mix of Puritan and Anglican Englishmen. Lower Rhine German groups of dissenting Amish and Mennonites, attracted by the religious toleration of Pennsylvania, settled in Germantown, Pennsylvania, as early as 1685. Located on the western edge of Philadelphia, the settlers and later German immigrants moved to the counties just further west in what would become Pennsylvania Dutch country.

The policies of the various other colonies tended to favor and encourage such group settlement to varying extents. In some cases, as in New Jersey, the fact that each community could decide what church would be supported by local taxes tended to attract coreligionists to specific communities. Thus in the colonial period, the counties of southern New Jersey (known in colonial times as West Jersey) tended to be dominated by Quakers, while townships in New Jersey closer to New York City were dominated by Lutheran, Dutch Reformed, and Anglican churches and settlers.

Ethnicity and religion divided the peoples of America, yet the official tolerance of religious diversity spawned a degree of mutual acceptance by one ethnic group of another. While crossreligious marriages were frowned upon, they were not prohibited, with individual families deciding which parents' church should be attended, if any. Modern descendants tracing their ancestry are sometimes astounded at the various strands of culture and religion that they find woven together.

To the south, Florida already had a rich Hispanic heritage, some of it filtered through Cuba. Smaller groups of immigrants from France and other countries in Europe were supplemented during the American Revolution by enthusiastic supporters of the idea of a republican experiment in the New World.

All of the thirteen colonies had the institution of African slavery, and people of African ancestry, both slave and free, constituted as much as 40 percent of the population of colonies like Georgia and South Carolina. In a wave of acts of emancipation, slaves living in the New England colonies were freed in the years right after the Revolution, soon joined by those in Pennsylvania, New York, and New Jersey. Although some African Americans in the south were free by birth or manumission, emancipation for 90 percent of those living south of Pennsylvania would have to wait until the years of the Civil War, 1861–65. Forcibly captured and transported under terrible conditions overland and across the ocean, Africans came from dozens of different linguistic stocks. Despite the disruptions of the middle passage, African Americans retained elements of their separate cultures, including some language and language patterns, and aspects of diet, religion, family, and music.

Native Americans, like African Americans, found themselves excluded from most of the rights of citizenship in the new Republic. In the Ohio and Mississippi Valley, many Native Americans resisted the advance of the European-descended settlers. In Florida, Creeks and Seminoles provided haven to escaped slaves, and together, they fought the encroachment of settlers. Some of the African Americans living with the Seminoles and other tribes moved west with them on the Trail of Tears to Indian Territory in what later became the state of Oklahoma. Other groups, like the Lumbees of North Carolina, stayed put, gradually adjusting to the new society around them. Throughout scattered rural communities, clusters of biracial and triracial descendents could trace their roots to Native-American and African ancestors, as well as to the English and Scotch-Irish.

The Louisiana Purchase brought the vast Mississippi Valley into the United States, along with the cosmopolitan city of New Orleans, where French exiles from Canada had already established a strong "Creole" culture. With the annexation of Texas, and following the Mexican-American War (1846–48), the United States incorporated as citizens hundreds of thousands of people of Hispanic ancestry. Individuals and communities in Texas and

New Mexico preserve not only their religion, but also their language, cuisine, customs, and architecture.

As the United States expanded to the west, with vast opportunities for settlement, waves of European immigrants contributed to the growth of the country, with liberal naturalization laws allowing immigrants to establish themselves as citizens. Following the revolutions of 1848 in Europe, and famines in Ireland, new floods of immigrants from Central Europe, Ireland, and Scandinavia all settled in pockets.

By the late 19th century, America had become a refuge for political and economic refugees, as well as enterprising families and individuals from many countries. More geographic-ethnic centers emerged, as new immigrants sought out friends and families who had already arrived, and settled near them. Neighborhoods and whole states took on some aspects of the ethnic cultures that the immigrants brought with them, with Italians settling in New York City, San Francisco, and New Jersey; Azoreans and continental Portuguese in Rhode Island and southern Massachusetts; Scandinavians in Wisconsin and Minnesota; Germans in Missouri; and Chinese and Japanese in a number of West Coast cities and towns. San Francisco and Boston became known for their Irish settlers, and Italians joined Franco-Hispanic Catholics of New Orleans. In some other scattered communities, such as the fishing port of Monterey, California, later Portuguese and Italian arrivals were also absorbed into the local Hispanic community, partly through the natural affinity of the shared Catholic faith.

As waves of immigrants continued to flow into the United States from the 1880s to World War I, the issue of immigration became even more politicized. On the one hand, older well-established ethnic communities sometimes resented the growing influence and political power of the new immigrants. Political machines in the larger cities made it a practice to incorporate the new settlers, providing them with some access to the politics and employment of city hall and at the same time expecting their votes and loyalty during election. The intricate interplay of ethnicity and politics through the late 19th century has been a rich field of historical research.

In the 1890s the United States suddenly acquired overseas territories, including Hawaii, and then Puerto Rico and Guam. Peoples from the new territories became American citizens, and although the great majority of them did not leave their islands, those who came to the continental United States became part of the increasingly diverse population. The tapestry of American culture and ancestry acquired new threads of Polynesian, Asian, Hispanic, and African-Hispanic people.

During the Progressive Era, American-born citizens of a liberal or progressive political inclination often had mixed feelings about immigrants. Some, with a more elitist set of values, believed that crime, alcoholism, and a variety of vices running from drug abuse through prostitution, gambling, and underground sports such as cockfighting, all could be traced to the new immigrants. The solution, they believed, would be "immigration reform": setting quotas that would restrict immigrants from all but Great Britain and northern Europe.

Other reformers took the position that the problems faced by new immigrants could be best dealt with through education, assistance, and social work. Still others approached the questions of poverty and adjustment of immigrants as part of the labor struggle, and believed that organizing through labor unions could bring pressure for better wages and working conditions. Meanwhile, immigrants continued to work through their churches, community organizations, and the complexities of American politics for recognition and rights.

Ultimately, two approaches emerged regarding how different ethnic groups would be viewed and how they would view themselves in America. For some, the idea of a "melting pot" had always held attraction. Under this way of thinking, all Americans would merge, with ethnic distinctions diminishing and the various cultures blending together to create a new American culture. Such a process of assimilation or integration appealed to many, both among American-born and immigrant groups. Others argued strongly that ethnic or racial identity should be preserved, with a sense of pride in heritage, so that America would continue to reflect its diversity, and so that particular groups would not forget their origins, traditions, and culture.

In 1882 the Chinese Exclusion Act prohibited further immigration of Chinese, and it was extended and made more restrictive in several amendments through 1902. Under the law, Chinese were prohibited from obtaining U.S. citizenship. In 1924 immigration legislation was enacted establishing quotas, based upon earlier census figures, so that the quotas favored those from Northern Europe. Under that law, Chinese were excluded, although between 1910 and 1940 more than 50,000 Chinese entered under claims they were returning or joining families already in the United States. The racial nature of the Chinese Exclusion and Immigration Acts tended to prevent the assimilation of Chinese into American society, with many cities, particularly in the west, developing defined Chinatowns or Chinese districts.

Whether an individual ethnic group should become homogenized, integrated, and assimilated into the total culture, or whether it should strive to maintain its own separate cultural identity, was often hotly debated. For some, like the Chinese, Native Americans, and African Americans, armed power of the state, law, and social discrimination tended to create and enforce separate communities and locales. For others, self-segregation and discrimination by other ethnic groups, and the natural process of settling near relatives and coreligionists led to definable ethnic regions and neighborhoods. Among such diverse groups as African Americans, Asians, Hispanics, Italians, Arab Americans, and Native Americans, leaders and spokesmen have debated the degree to which cultural identity should be sacrificed in the name of assimilation. In the 21st century, the debates have continued, sometimes with great controversy. At other times, the dialogues went on almost unnoticed by the rest of the country.

Armed conflict, race-wars, reservation policy, segregation, exclusion, and detention camps in time of war have shown the harsh and ugly side of enforced separation. Even though the multiethnic and multicultural heritage of the United States has been fraught with crisis and controversy, it has also been a source of strength. With roots in so many cultures and with the many struggles to establish and maintain social justice, America has also represented some of the best aspirations of humanity to live in peace with one another. The search for social equity has been difficult, but the fact that the effort has continued for more than two centuries is in itself an achievement.

In this series on Multicultural America, each volume is dedicated to the history of one ethnocultural group, tracing through time the struggles against discrimination and for fair play, as well as the effort to preserve and cherish an independent cultural heritage.

THE ARAB AMERICANS

Because Arabic is a language spoken with various accents and dialects in more than 20 countries, and because "Arabia" can either refer to the country of Saudi Arabia or to all of the countries of the Arabian Peninsula, tracing the origins of, and even defining Arab Americans presents numerous issues.

During World War I, the Ottoman Empire sided with Germany, Austria-Hungary, and Bulgaria as a member of the Central Powers. The empire was ruled by Turks from Turkey who spoke Turkish. The empire included many Arabic-speaking peoples in a wide region of the Middle East. That empire was broken up in 1918–19 after the defeat of the Central Powers by the Allies, with various parts of the empire parceled out as mandates (or protectorates), or as semi-sovereign or sovereign countries. On the Arabian Peninsula, the Arab Revolt against Ottoman rule brought grudging recognition from Britain, France, and the other Allies, of the claims to self-government of at least a part of the Arabian Peninsula.

Some of the former Ottoman Empire provinces, treated as League of Nations mandates for a period of years, later became independent, joining the League, or later joining the United Nations and receiving international recognition as sovereign nations. In addition, Arabic had spread beyond the borders of the Ottoman Empire in earlier centuries, across much of North and East Africa. As a result of these historic developments, today Arabic is the national language, or one of two major official languages, of the following nations or states: Algeria, Bahrain, Chad, Djibouti, Egypt, Eritrea, Iraq, Israel, Jordan, Kuwait, Lebanon, Libya, Mauritania, Morocco, Oman, Palestine, Qatar, Saudi Arabia, Somalia, Sudan, Syria, Tunisia, United Arab Emirates, and Yemen.

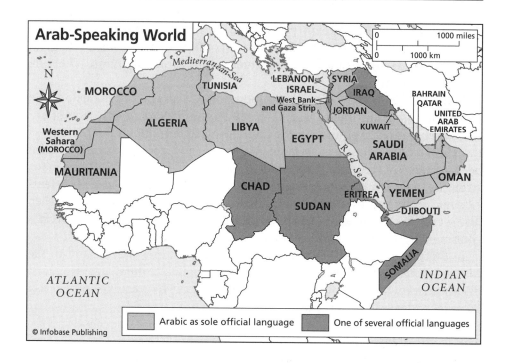

Arab-Speaking World

Arabic as sole official language   One of several official languages

© Infobase Publishing

Consequently, American immigration officials, the American press, and the American public were often unsure what terms to use to describe the various peoples from these places who entered the United States. For decades, many light-skinned Arabic-speaking peoples were simply categorized by immigration officials as "Syrian." Most came from the loosely defined "Levant," which includes Syria, Lebanon, Israel, Palestine, and Jordan, although smaller numbers came from all of the other nations listed above.

Divisions between Sunni and Shi'a Muslims, the cause of so much crisis and contention in contemporary Iraq, divided some Muslims who emigrated to the United States. Not all Arabic-speaking peoples were Muslims, either. Some were "ancient Christians," some were Druze, and others were Syrian Orthodox Christians or members of other Christian denominations. Today, an estimated 65 percent of Arab Americans are Christian and only 25 percent are Muslim. These factors not only confused the American immigration and census officials at the time, they made it difficult for historians and sociologists to unravel the numbers and movements of the various peoples speaking Arabic from the Middle East and North and East Africa who came to the United States.

Of more importance to people of Arab ancestry, the divisions and differences among the peoples tended to make it difficult for them and their descendants in the United States to develop effective political/social groups around which to develop defenses of rights. Although Islam brought some of these groups together, the fact that the majority of Arabic-speaking peoples coming to America were not Muslims made it much more difficult for Arabic-speaking peoples to use religion and houses of worship from which to establish their political and social networks.

Other cultural differences among the various Arabic-speaking peoples from different countries are profound. While some Yeminis and Saudis share close dialects of Arabic and the Wahabi (or Salafi) tradition of Sunni Islam, they find they have only a little in common with Lebanese, Moroccans, or Algerians, in language, faith, diet, and traditions.

A further complication derives from the fact that some immigrants from predominantly Arabic-speaking countries, such as Iraq, Syria, or parts of North Africa come from an entirely different, non-Arab cultural/linguistic heritage, such as the Kurds, Circassians, or Berbers. While immigration officials and others might think of them as Arabs, such peoples were well aware that their history, language, and culture set them clearly apart from that group.

The divisions also stood in the way of establishing geographic/cultural enclaves, and using those enclaves or clusters to operate in the American political system. Since the U.S. federal republican structure is built to represent states or districts, the natural tendency of various groups to settle together has given some ethnic-cultural groups greater clout as they could elect local county and city officials, send legislators to state legislatures, and effectively throw their support behind specific members of Congress. Many self-defined ethnic communities, because of their concentration in particular states and counties, have been able to send representatives of their ethnic group to Congress. Despite the many barriers to forming communities, Arab neighborhoods did develop in Michigan, California, New Jersey, and scattered other locations where the Arab vote had some effect. Unraveling this intricate and fascinating story over the decades since the 19th century is the subject of this volume.

RODNEY CARLISLE
GENERAL EDITOR

CHAPTER 1

Beginnings in America: Precolonial to 1900

ARAB AMERICANS CAN trace their heritage to about 22 different countries in Africa and Asia, where long ago (around 10,000 to 8,000 B.C.E.) humankind first formed settled societies. The people cultivated crops, raised livestock, and established cities where different skills and occupations were promoted. Civilization's first signs are found in Africa—most specifically Egypt—and in the Middle East, most famously the Fertile Crescent within modern-day Iraq. The first city known to exist, Jericho, is found in the Jordan Rift Valley, or the modern-day West Bank. These locations are part of the contemporary Arab world.

Arabia was once considered to be a peninsula of southwest Asia between the Red Sea and the Persian Gulf (modern-day Saudi Arabia). It included Saudi Arabia, Yemen, Oman, the United Arab Emirates, Qatar, Bahrain, and Kuwait. Today, "Arabia" (the Arab homeland) covers some 5,000 miles, from the Atlantic coast in northwest Africa to the Arabian Sea in the east, and from Central Africa in the south to the Mediterranean Sea in the north. Seventy-two percent of its territory lies in Africa, and 28 percent lies in Asia. The countries comprising the Arabian homeland today are Algeria, Bahrain, the Comoros Islands, Djibouti, Egypt, Iraq, Jordan, Kuwait, Lebanon, Libya, Mauritania, Morocco, Oman, Palestine, Qatar, Saudi Arabia, Somalia, Sudan, Syria, Tunisia, the United Arab Emirates, and Yemen.

1

The vast geographical area of "Arabia" is home to many diverse cultures and peoples of different ethnicities, appearances, political systems, and religious beliefs. In *Arabs in America: Building a New Future,* Suad Joseph writes: "There are Palestinians, Iraqis, Kuwaitis, Yemenis, Saudi Arabians, Bahreinis, Qataris, Duabis, Egyptians, Libyans, Tunisians, Moroccans, Algerians, Sudanese, Eritreans, and Mauritanians; there are Maronites, Catholics, Protestants, Greek Orthodox, Jews, Sunnis, Shi'a, Druze, Sufis, Alawites, Nestorians, Assyrians, Copts, Chaldeans, and Bahais; there are Berbers, Kurds, Armenians, Bedu, Gypsies and many others with different languages, religions, ethnic, and national identifications and cultures who are all congealed as Arab in popular representation whether or not those people may identify as Arab."

The religion of Islam and the Arabic language remain the Arab world's two predominant cultural features, although six countries with the largest Muslim populations (Indonesia, Pakistan, Bangladesh, India, Turkey, and Iran) are not Arab countries. Not all Muslims are Arab, and not all Arabs are Muslim. Who, then, is an Arab? An Arab is: a person who comes from or whose ancestors come from countries comprising the Arab homeland, initially originating from a peninsula in southwest Asia; speaks the Arabic language or a derivative of it; shares common heritage, history, and traditions; and considers himself or herself to be an Arab. Arab Americans are those who have either been born in the United States or have become U.S. citizens, and have family ties to the peoples of Arabia (the Arab homeland). About three million Arab Americans live in the United States today.

EARLY CONTACTS

Up through the 21st century, there were two major waves of Arab immigration to America: from the 1870s to World War II, and from World War II to September 11, 2001. But prior to 1859, contact was sporadic. Charles Michael Boland, in his book *They All Discovered America* and Joseph Ayoob of Alquippa in his writings *Were the Phoenicians the First to Discover America?* proposed that a group of Phoenicians (people of modern Lebanon) were blown off course during a ship expedition to Ultima Thule (Iceland) between 480 B.C.E. and 146 B.C.E. Some have speculated that hewn stones and inscriptions found near Pattee's Caves in North Salem, New Hampshire, and in Pennsylvania near Mechanicsburg are proof of their presence in North America. Other evidence also suggests that individual Muslims may have come to North American shores with exploring expeditions in the 1100s. According to the Arab geographer al-Sherif al-Idrisi, eight adventurous Arabs set sail from Lisbon, Portugal, and landed in South America before 1492. Christopher Columbus had Idrisi's book with him when he sailed to America for the first time.

In 1539 an expedition into territories now known as New Mexico and Arizona was headed by Franciscan Friar Marcos de Niza, who was accompanied by Estephan (also spelled Estevanico), his Moroccan Arab guide. And in 1668 Father Elias al-Mawsili of Mosul, Iraq made an extensive journey through Mexico and Central and South America. His travels were recorded in Arabic in the book *Rihlat Awwal Sharqi Ila Amrika* (The Trip of the First Easterner to America).

THE SLAVE TRADE AND THE AMERICAN REVOLUTION
The first large group of Muslims to arrive in America were brought as slaves from the West African territories now known as Ghana, the Ivory Coast, Niger, Burkina Faso, and Algeria between 1530 and 1851. Historians estimate that between 14 and 30 percent of all slaves in the United States were Muslims. In 1717 Arabic-speaking slaves arrived with the slave trade in the American colonies. They used the words "Allah" and "Muhammad," refused to eat pork, and went by names such as Omar Ibn Said, Job Ben Solomon, Paul Lahman Kibby, Prince Omar, and Ben Ali. Many African Americans today have rediscovered these connections to Arabic culture and the religion of Islam.

During the American Revolution, it has been reported that the Continental Congress negotiated with Algeria to import horses for General George Washington's army. In 1777 Morocco was the first country to formally recognize the newly declared independence of the United States of America. However, in 1784, the first American ship was seized by Moroccan pirates. These raiders, who would capture ships and enslave the crews, had become

Peter Salem (or Saleem), a former slave believed to be Muslim like an estimated 30 percent of African-American slaves, was a hero of the Battle of Bunker Hill in the Revolutionary War. He is depicted at the far right of this painting partially obscured behind an Anglo-American soldier.

known as the Barbary pirates. Nautical traders from the United States became frequent victims of the Barbary pirates as soon as the United States began trading with Europe and refused to pay the required tribute to North African states. Slave-taking persisted into the 19th century. It was not until 1815 that naval victories in the Barbary Wars ended tribute payments by the United States.

In 1786 Mr. Thomas Barclay, the first American ambassador to Morocco, had negotiated the Treaty of Friendship and Cooperation between Mohammed III, king of Morocco at that time and George Washington, the first U.S. president. The document signed and circulated on June 23, 1786 officially recognized the United States as an independent nation. It attested to the friendship and cooperation between the two nations and allowed free passage through Moroccan waters to all American ships. On July 18, 1787, the document was ratified by the U.S. Congress, and a letter of thanks was sent to Morocco's king, also asking that he assist in mediation between the United States and the rulers of Tripoli and Tunisia.

For the next 70 years, contact between Arabs and Americans was infrequent and varied. In 1790 South Carolina's House of Representatives mandated that "Sundry Free Moors, Subjects of the Emperor of Morocco," be tried in their courts according to the laws pertaining to citizens of South Carolina, and not under the codes for African Americans.

THE EARLY 19th CENTURY

The Census Bureau, which was one medium by which race and racism was defined, reveals how in the United States the meaning of "race" has changed according to historical perspective, as well as political and social circumstances. In 1790 the Census Bureau divided the U.S. population into the racial categories of "free whites," "slaves," and "all other free persons" (i.e.: American Indians). The census added "free colored persons" to the racial categories in 1820. This left the door open for those with darker complexions and later those originating from Asia and other parts of the world who could not be otherwise classified. Those with Arab ancestry may have been classified in this new category; however, according to their skin color, they may also have been classified as a "free white." In 1850 the 7th Federal Census of the United States provided the skin-color choices of "white," "black," or "mulatto." The United States has, at different times, classified Arab immigrants as African, Asian, white, European, or as belonging to a separate group. Most Arab Americans identify more closely with nationality than with ethnic group. For Arab Americans, classification became complex.

Among the contacts between Arab and American cultures during this era was the 1840 visit of the ship *al-Sultanah*, which arrived with cargo at New York harbor after being sent by Sayyid Said Bin Sultan, ruler of Muscat (Muscat and Oman today), as part of a trade treaty with the United States. Newspapers gave frequent accounts of the three-month visit, and a picture of the ship's commander, Al-Haj Ahmad Bin Na'aman, still hangs in the offices of the Art Commission in New York City's City Hall. In 1848 Father Flavianus Kfoury, a Melkite Catholic priest, entered the United States on a mission to gain financial support in the rebuilding of St. John's Convent in Khonchara in present-day Lebanon. Bishop John Hughes of New York provided him with letters of introduction in his travels around the United States, asking others to assist the Syrian priest during his two-year stay.

Other visitors included a young Syrian named Antonio Bishallany, who came to study at the Amenia Seminary in New York in 1854. He died within two years, however, and never returned to minister in Syria as planned. His body was buried in Brooklyn, New York. Gregory Wortabet, an American who was the assistant to the American Missionaries in Beirut, came to America in 1855 for a short stay and then returned to Syria. In 1856 and 1857, cargos of 33 and 44 camels, accompanied by two Turks and three Arabs from the Near East, arrived at Indianola, Texas, for service in the U.S. Army in the southwest. One of the Arabs became well known for his handling of the animals, and went by his nickname "Hadgi Ali," which southwesterners pronounced "Hi Jolly."

Such contact did not, however, constitute large groups of Arabs immigrating to the United States. The few early Arab immigrants were isolated individual settlers, primarily Christians from the Ottoman province of Syria, especially the Mount Lebanon region. A few early immigrants came from Palestine or other regions, and a few were of the Muslim or Druze faiths. The Druze are a sect with their own interpretation of the Qur'an. It is difficult to estimate the number of Arabs who may have immigrated to America in family groups between precolonial times and the late 19th century, because U.S. immigration statistics classified all Arabs, including the predominant Syrians, as being from "Turkey in Asia" until 1899, when the classification "Syrian" was added.

THE FIRST WAVE OF ARAB IMMIGRATION

Arabs were still a minority in the overall surge of immigration to the United States in the late 19th and early 20th centuries. The first wave of Arab immigrants to the United States lasted from the late 1870s to 1924 and peaked during World War I. Until 1909 Arab Americans were generally classified as whites, allowing them to naturalize more easily, hold political office, and own property. Many Arabic names also became Americanized due to Americans' difficulty with Arabic pronunciation and spelling. A lack of clear and reliable statistics makes exact calculations impossible, but approximately 100,000 Arab Americans lived in the United States by 1914.

New York was the most common port of arrival, but others came through New Orleans, Boston, Philadelphia, Baltimore, or other ports. Still others

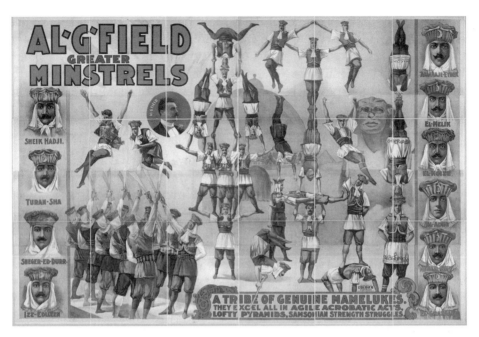

This poster for a performance portraying Egyptian acrobats by a company that also ran blackface minstrel shows that stereotyped African Americans was printed in New York around 1900. It suggests both Americans' growing familiarity with Arab cultures, and the potential for ethnic stereotyping.

came across the Canadian or Mexican borders, or immigrated to other countries and later continued their journey to the United States. The earliest immigrants tended to be young, single men. Those early arrivals who were married usually left their families behind, sometimes sending for them later. Christian women, both married and single, began arriving later, while few Muslim married women came. There is no evidence of single Muslim women among early immigrants. Most were poorly educated farmers or artisans with enough money to secure their passage. The majority emigrated voluntarily in order to achieve economic success in "Amerka," and eventually return to their home villages with enhanced wealth and prestige. Many early immigrants also came for the adventure. Lesser reasons for emigrating included overpopulation, land shortages, family problems, avoidance of taxes or military service, and a silkworm blight. A small handful of intellectuals arrived in America after the Turkish government began suppressing freedom of the press in the 1880s. Acceptance of America as a final destination did not come until late in the first wave of Arab immigration.

Arab Americans quickly found work as factory workers, farmers, or peddlers. The economic successes of early immigrants fueled a chain migration of other family members or residents from their home villages. Others were attracted by industries, steamship companies, and railroads that advertised overseas to attract potential workers, or by the stories of overseas missionaries they met in their native villages. Thus a network of aid developed along the main immigration routes, and most immigrants arrived in the United States with a destination in mind and a friend or relative to meet.

CULTURAL CHARACTERISTICS AND NEIGHBORHOOD LIFE

Muslim immigrants primarily settled in large industrial cities, while the Christians and Druze were more dispersed. Most Druze settled in Virginia, West Virginia, Kentucky, Tennessee, and Washington. Syrians resided in neighborhoods, known as *haras*, based on their home country's religious sect and place of origin, where different sects or villages often had their own customs and institutions. Syrians identified themselves by sect or place of origin, rather than by nationality, and settled accordingly. Arab Americans recreated the interdependence of village life in America, and the recruitment of new immigrants usually occurred along family or village lines. Arab-American sects and neighborhoods usually cooperated with one another, but sectarian factionalism was also common, and there was no real sense of a unified, national identity.

The largest Arab-American colony was in New York City on Manhattan's lower west side along Washington Street, which became known as Little Syria. Little Syria was a temporary starting point for some new arrivals, while others made it their final destination. Its larger size made it more heterogeneous than most Arab-American settlements. Little Syria featured paved streets, brownstone row homes, coffeehouses, factories, grocery stores, and other Arab-American-owned businesses. Little Syria and other urban areas were noted for their noise and activity. A network of settlements extended from Little Syria, and eventually could be found throughout the country. Boarding houses were a common feature of most Syrian communities due to the high number of single men among Arab Americans. Family homes were often crowded, holding up to three generations, and offered little privacy.

Arab-American immigrants usually wore traditional village-style dress upon their arrival in the United States, but quickly began adopting Western-style dress. Traditional Syrian everyday wear for women included a long, ankle-length, loose-fitting

In this artist's depiction of a street scene in Little Syria, peddlers are setting out with their wares.

skirt and blouse, and a shawl or kerchief over the hair. Traditional Syrian everyday wear for men included a garment similar to a dress and a waist sash, or a baggy white collarless shirt, black vest, and baggy black trousers with narrow ankles. Men usually wore a fringed headscarf for everyday wear, or a dressier red felt hat with a black tassel, similar to a fez, for special occasions. Urban peddlers of expensive items often wore serge suits and shined their shoes. The few Muslim women in the United States veiled themselves or covered their hair while in public in accordance to religious custom.

Food played a large role in Arab, and subsequently Arab-American culture. Many Arab women cooked traditional dishes using ingredients imported from their homelands. Diet staples included rice, crushed wheat (*burghul*), barley, lentils, flat leavened bread, and a variety of fruits and vegetables. Fish or meat, usually lamb, was served occasionally. Middle Eastern herbs provided flavoring. Turkish coffee was a popular beverage. Favorite dishes included *kibbie*, made with lean lamb; and burghul and *mjaddarra*, a common lentil dish. Recipes were passed down from generation to generation, and even those Arab Americans who did not speak Arabic often knew the Arabic words for popular food dishes. Food was an avenue through which Arab Americans could demonstrate their hospitality and generosity, and large feasts often accompanied celebrations or parties (*haflas*).

In addition to formal celebrations such as weddings, Arab Americans enjoyed informal social gatherings. Many immigrants brought traditional musical instruments such as the *oud*, a fretless stringed instrument. Musicians and singers performed traditional village songs at informal musical gatherings known as *sahras*, accompanied by dancing. Such gatherings would become important fundraising events for religious and social organizations. Women enjoyed visiting with one another at home, while men enjoyed gathering in restaurants or coffee shops to play backgammon, drink Turkish coffee, smoke water pipes, and discuss business. Even traveling peddlers would occasionally meet at town hotels or boarding houses to exchange news and pleasantries.

Many first-wave immigrants came to the United States only to work for a period of time and return home. Thus, it took several decades before first-wave Arab Americans formed their own social, political, and religious institutions. Once a sense of permanence took hold in the 1890s, stable communities and institutions began

Nineteenth-century Arab-American immigrants introduced instruments like this oud to the United States.

Kawkub Amrika (Star of America)

Syrian immigrants Najib and Ibrahim Arbeely founded the *Kawkub Amrika* (Star of America) in 1892. Najib and Ibrahim were the sons of Dr. Joseph Arbeely, who had been president of the Greek Orthodox Patriarchal College in Damascus before immigrating to the United States. Najib Arbeely also served as a U.S. consul to Jerusalem, and as an Arabic translator and physician for the Bureau of Immigration at Ellis Island in New York City. Ibrahim Arbeely was also a practicing pediatric physician and published an English-Arabic primer to teach English and American social customs to Arab immigrants. *Kawkub Amrika* was the first Arabic-language newspaper published in the United States, and was printed on the first Arabic linotype-printing machine in New York. It was an important first step in the development of Arab-American institutions.

A front page of the Kawkub Amrika *paper bearing the calligraphy logo and star and crescent sign.*

The first issue of the *Kawkub Amrika* appeared on April 15, 1892, and ran for 15 years, a long run considering that many early Arab-American institutions were short-lived. It was a weekly paper featuring three Arabic pages, and one English page that was soon dropped. The banner featured the paper's logo in Arabic calligraphy, as well as the star and crescent sign of the Ottoman Empire, making it easily recognizable to Arab Americans. Its columns featured general news of the United States and the Middle East, as well as Arabic poems and literary pieces, reader letters, and advertisements. The paper also played an important role in the adjustment of new immigrants by covering American politics, news, and customs, and promoting assimilation. Later competitors included *al-Ayam* (The Days), which began appearing in 1897, and *al-Hoda* (The Guidance), which began appearing in 1898.

appearing. Most institutions developed in the more populous urban centers, especially New York City's Little Syria neighborhood. An Arabic-language press began operating in 1892 with the founding of the newspaper *Kawkub Amrika* (Star of America) in New York City by Najib and Ibrahim Arbeely. *Al-Ayam* and *al-Hoda* were other popular newspapers. These papers carried news from home, literary pieces, and discussions of political and social issues such as whether women should work. The Arab press in America also urged immigrants to naturalize and assimilate, offering books to help them navigate the process. Many of the publishers and editors became community leaders. A few women wrote for the Arab-American press, including renowned journalist Afifa Karam, who began writing for *al-Hoda* in 1899 at the age of 16. Other institutions included educational and charitable associations and churches. The Syrian Society, organized by Dr. Ameen F. Haddad in 1892, taught English and industrial skills. The Syrian Women's Union of New York, established in 1896, aided the poor, held sewing circles, and provided a nursery for working mothers.

RELIGION AND VALUES

The majority of Arab Americans who arrived in the first wave of immigration were Christians, most belonging to the Maronite, Melkite, or Syrian Orthodox sects. Maronites were the largest sect. Maronites and Melkites, affiliated with the Vatican, often worshipped in Roman Catholic churches, while Syrian Orthodox Christians often worshipped with other Orthodox sects, such as Greek and Russian Orthodox. A few immigrants were Roman Catholic or belonged to various Protestant sects, having been converted by missionaries before their arrival in America. Early clergy were mostly itinerant preachers. The relatively small number of early Arab migrants meant that they did not establish their own parishes until the 1890s, when a sense of permanent residence in the United States became more widespread. These churches would become centers of community activity. Muslims and Druze made up less than 10 percent of first wave Arab immigrants; few mosques would be built in the United States until the 1920s.

Syrian immigrants emphasized the importance of industriousness, thrift, and resourcefulness in order to achieve their economic goals. They were generally willing to take risks and endure hardships and self-sacrifice in order to improve their social and economic standing, both in the United States and in their villages back home. Arab Americans also valued the family over the individual, and emphasized the importance of family unity, honor, and loyalty. Many earned money to improve not only their own social and economic status, but also that of their families. For example, many sent monetary remittances to family back home to repay debts or mortgages, or to finance the passage of relatives to America. Those immigrants who struggled found assistance among their fellow Arab Americans, as charity was an important avenue for the expression of the cultural and religious values of aid, generosity, and hospitality. Thus few Arab Americans had to rely on outside institutions for help.

Older immigrants paved the way for the newly arrived, easing hardships by sharing their experiences. Neighbors and family members learned to read and write Arabic and speak English. For older immigrants, settling into marriage and family life became increasingly important, as greater numbers decided to make America their permanent home. Many immigrants traveled home to marry, attend to economic or family obligations, or simply to visit friends and relatives. Men and women were expected to marry for cultural and economic reasons, and matchmakers frequently targeted single Arab Americans. The disproportionate number of men necessitated that many men return home to find brides often selected for them by parents or relatives. Wives were expected to respect and aid their husbands, and divorce was extremely rare. Sexual topics were taboo for women. Sectarian identification was very important, so there were few interfaith marriages. Those who did marry outside their faith were frequently ostracized.

ECONOMIC LIFE

Economic opportunity was the main motivation for Arab immigration during the first wave, and Arab Americans were known for their hard work and ambition. International expositions, such as the 1876 Philadelphia Centennial Exposition and the World's Columbian Exposition in Chicago in 1893, introduced Arab products to Americans and showed Arab businessmen the profits to be made in America. Common jobs included peddling, storekeeping, factory work, manufacturing, banking, and farming. A few Arab-American families earned enough to establish their own businesses, such as the Merhiges and Bardawills, who flourished in the silk and linen industries; and the Faour brothers, who opened the first Arab-owned bank in the United States and supplied credit to fellow Arab Americans. The Faours became one of the wealthiest Arab-American families in the United States by the end of the 19th century.

A demonstration of a traditional Middle Eastern sedan chair at the 1893 World's Columbian Exposition in Chicago.

World Fairs, Culture, and Trade

Many historians credit the 1876 Philadelphia Centennial Exposition, officially known as the International Exposition of Arts, Manufactures, and Products of the Soil and Mine, with the launching of the first wave of Arab immigration to the United States. It was the first large-scale world fair to be held in the United States. The exposition, celebrating the 100-year anniversary of the signing of the Declaration of Independence, was designed to showcase American mechanical and industrial knowledge, but also featured exhibits from around the world. The Sultan of the Ottoman Empire, Abdul Hamid II, accepted the organizers' invitation to establish an exhibit at the exposition. Over 1,500 Arab and Turkish firms and entrepreneurs attended.

Millions of visitors explored the exhibits in more than 200 buildings on over 71 acres in Fairmount Park along the Schuylkill River. The Arab and Turkish vendors sold cotton, coffee, olivewood rosaries and crosses carved in Jerusalem, ceramic vases, gold filigree and amber jewelry, spices, nuts, perfumes, and artwork. The most popular exhibits included a Moroccan booth displaying traditional arts and crafts, and a Tunisian café serving coffee, sweets, and Turkish water pipes. Some of the tradesmen who exhibited their wares at the exposition found it so lucrative that they stayed in America to establish import businesses. Those who returned home spread stories of the possible wealth to be had in America, fueling the first wave of immigrants. Other key expositions included Chicago in 1893, and St. Louis in 1906.

An Egyptian dancer at the World's Columbian Exposition in Chicago around 1893. A series of large world fairs in the late 1800s were watershed events for crosscultural exposure and trade.

Arab Americans' emphasis on family meant that employment was often a family enterprise. For example, women and children often peddled along with their husbands, and family-owned stores often employed only family members and had living quarters upstairs. Arab-American women also worked in the textile mills and factories that proliferated during the Industrial Revolution of the mid- to late-19th century. Others sewed or crocheted items to be sold by their husbands. Some Arab Americans ran their own warehouses, mills, and import businesses. A silk industry, popular back home in Syria, developed in New York and New Jersey. Potential farmers were attracted by the offer of Midwestern land under the federal Homestead Act of 1862. Taking in boarding peddlers was yet another possible economic enterprise.

PEDDLING LIFE

Peddling became the most common occupation among early Arab immigrants because it was particularly suited to their desire for independence and their ambition to quickly make money and return home. It was also an easy occupation in which to start due to the limited need for training or the ability to speak English. Pack peddling, in which the peddler carried his supplies in cases and traveled long distances in rural America by foot, was the most common. Other types of peddling included pushcart peddling, in which a merchandise cart was wheeled through urban streets on a daily basis. Those peddlers who traveled shorter distances over the same routes developed a loyal customer base and often sold on credit. Almost all Arab Americans in this period participated in the peddling trade at some point in their working lives, although it was most common among the Syrians. Even those who felt it was undignified could turn to it as a safety valve in times of trouble. Peddling was also appealing because it offered relative independence compared to factory work, and provided more opportunities to earn cash.

Most newcomers received training and saleable goods from suppliers, who played a vital role in the peddling industry. Rudimentary training included a few words of English, packing instructions, methods of attracting customers' interests, and dealing with American currency and the licenses required in many areas. Suppliers also offered credit to new arrivals, held savings, recommended merchandising routes, ran boarding houses, settled quarrels and disputes with local authorities, and offered advice on the naturalization process. Suppliers settled in towns with potential markets and often knew of coal, oil, or gold discoveries. By 1900 a network of peddling settlements developed across the country. These settlements served as places to re-supply, visit friends and relatives, and relax. Little Syria in New York City served as a model for other settlements and was the major supplier of goods to be merchandised. Other large settlements existed in Fort Wayne, Indiana and Spring Valley, Illinois. Cedar Rapids, Iowa was home to one of earliest continuously occupied Muslim communities.

Peddlers carried their wares in wooden or leather cases known as *qash-sha* and in heavy packs. The main customers were women, whose interests determined which items peddlers would carry. Common dry goods included sewing supplies, cotton fabrics, silks, lace-trimmed sheets and pillowcases, trimmings, jewelry, combs, picture frames, mirrors, and trinkets and knick-knacks of various kinds. Clothing items included scarves, dress collars, handkerchiefs, underwear, garters, suspenders, and gloves and caps for laborers. Toiletries included perfumes, shaving soaps, straight razors, powder, and lotions. Holy Land items, such as crucifixes, rosaries, and Orthodox icons were among the first items to be peddled, and were particularly valuable stock as they were popular items. City peddlers draped them on their arms or a stick to attract sales. Some later peddlers began specializing in more expensive wares such as Oriental rugs and fine imported linens and laces. Bartering was common in the peddling trade.

The Peddlers' Settlement at Fort Wayne, Indiana

Fort Wayne, Indiana, a commercial, industrial city in close proximity to the Pennsylvania Railroad, was home to one of the larger Syrian communities in the United States in the late 1800s. The founder of the Syrian community, Salem Bashara, was born in Dahr al-Ahmar not far from Damascus and came to the United States along with his two brothers on his father's second trip to America in 1887. By 1890 Salem had purchased a building housing multiple stores, and had become a major supplier to area peddlers. Salem Bashara is one of the better-known examples of the vital role suppliers played in helping new arrivals adjust to life in America. The peddlers' settlement at Fort Wayne became a prototype for other settlements that would follow.

In his role as supplier, Salem Bashara often met new immigrant arrivals as they stepped off the train. He then provided them with the information and supplies they needed, often on credit, to get started in the peddling business. Most of the Syrian immigrants who came to Fort Wayne were of the Orthodox sect, and most were from the villages of Rashayya and Aytha. The practice of settling with other immigrants of the same sect or place of origin was common among Arab Americans at the time. Fort Wayne grew to become one of the largest and most successful of the peddling settlements by the turn of the century. As peddling gradually diminished as a profession at the beginning of the 20th century, Fort Wayne's once-flourishing Syrian community also dwindled. Salem Bashara sold his business around 1906 and died before 1910.

This street peddler lifts his ornamented tea urn onto his back with a strap as he doles out drinks to customers in Little Syria in New York City around 1900.

After packing their cases, peddlers would depart in pairs or small groups, covering different territories in informal arrangements that prevented competition. These groups would then separate and meet every so often for safety and companionship. Women peddlers stayed in groups and were accompanied by men if they were to cover long distances. Many peddlers traveled for days, weeks, or months between various rural and town markets, while others peddled in the larger cities on a daily basis and returned home each evening. On weekends, peddlers would often meet at a prearranged boarding house or hotel where they could eat, browse the town stores, share their experiences, shave and take a bath, and perhaps enjoy some entertainment.

Pack peddlers, who traveled many miles for up to six months at a time, endured weather extremes such as heat or freezing temperatures, blisters from excessive walking, sore muscles from the heavy weight of their packs, fatigue, hunger, thirst, wet and dirty clothing, and loneliness. At the end of the day, peddlers on the road would find an open space or abandoned building to sleep or ask for food and lodgings at a farmhouse, often repaying the hospitality with the gift of some small notion from his pack. Those peddlers who slept in the open were constantly vigilant against thieves and stray animals. Some also had to overcome language barriers, cultural misunderstandings, prejudices, and the sometimes excessive licensing fees instigated by town merchants, who often viewed the peddlers as a threat to their businesses. Some peddlers purchased a horse and buggy for ease of travel and a greater selection of merchandise.

PEDDLING AND ASSIMILATION

Historian Alixa Naff notes that peddling played a vital role in the assimilation of early Arab immigrants into American society. American reaction to Arab-American peddlers ranged from hostility, to curiosity, to friendliness. Newspaper and journal articles from the period described their appearances and customs with curiosity and occasional ridicule. While their darker skin and native dress made them more conspicuous during a time of rising anti-immigrant feelings, Arab Americans were able to escape the systematic prejudice faced by groups such as the Chinese because they remained relatively small in number and geographically dispersed. Most peddlers relied on humor and determination to put incidents of discrimination behind them.

Peddlers used their work as a way to learn English, explore the landscape, and pick up regional and national customs as they interacted with their customers, often through a mixture of broken English and hand signals. Eventually Syrian Americans spoke in a combination of Arabic and English. Peddling provided a key service to housebound immigrants or isolated farm wives, and drove the economic success of early Arab Americans. A peddler could make an average annual income of $1,000–$2,000, more than the average income for an industrial worker. Peddling largely disappeared by 1910 as better transportation, the Sears catalog, and dime stores like Woolworth's lured customers elsewhere.

CONCLUSION

The early groups of Arab-American immigrants, like those who followed, transferred the importance of family, marriage, and children to their new country, attempting to maintain the interconnectedness of the Arab family in their lives in the United States. These immigrants set the pattern of moving to neighborhoods or suburbs that were close to people from their families, villages, or cities of origin. Traditional networks were later expanded to include other Arabs who were not from their family or neighborhood in order to maintain traditions among people who understood their customs. These settlements and networks would change over the next century, but a number would grow into significant communities in the same areas of the country where small numbers of early immigrants originally set down roots.

DENISE HINDS-ZAAMI
PENNSYLVANIA STATE UNIVERSITY
MARCELLA BUSH TREVINO
BARRY UNIVERSITY

Further Reading

Abraham, Nabeel and Sameer Y. Abraham, eds. *Arabs in the New World: Studies on Arab American Communities*. Detroit, MI: Wayne State University Center for Urban Ethnic Studies, 1983.

Benson, Kathleen and Philip Kayal, eds. *A Community of Many Worlds: Arab Americans in New York City*. New York: Museum of the City of New York and Syracuse University Press, 2002.

Boosahda, Elizabeth. *Arab American Faces and Voices: The Origins of an Immigrant Community*. Austin, TX: University of Texas Press, 2003.

Hooglund, Eric J. *Crossing the Waters: Arabic-Speaking Immigrants to the United States Before 1940*. Washington, D.C.: Smithsonian Institution Press, 1987.

Jamal, Amaney and Nadine Naber, eds. *Race and Arab Americans Before and After 9/11: From Invisible Citizens to Visible Subjects*. Syracuse, NY: Syracuse University Press, 2008.

Koszegi, Michael and J. Gordon Melton. *Islam in North America: A Sourcebook*. New York: Garland Publications, 1992.

Marvasti, Amir B. and Kayrn D. McKinney. *Middle Eastern Lives in America*. Lanham, MD: Rowman and Littlefield Publishers, Inc., 2004.

Mehdi, Beverlee Turner. *The Arabs in America, 1492–1977: A Chronology and Fact Book*. Dobbs Ferry, NY: Oceana Publications, 1978.

Miller, Sally M., ed. *The Ethnic Press in the United States*. Westport, CT: Greenwood Press, 1987.

Naff, Alixa. *Becoming American: The Early Arab Immigrant Experience*. Carbondale, IL: Southern Illinois University Press, 1985.

Oren, Michael B. "The Middle East and the Making of the United States 1776 to 1815." *Columbia News* (November 16, 2005). Columbia University. Available online, URL: www.columbia.edu. Accessed November 2008.

Orfalea, Gregory. *The Arab Americans: A History*. Northampton, MA: Olive Branch Press, 2006.

———. *Before the Flames: A Quest for the History of Arab Americans*. Austin, TX: University of Texas Press, 1988.

Prewitt, Kenneth. "Demography, Diversity, and Democracy: The 2000 Census Story." *Brookings Review*, Vol. 20, No. 1, winter 2002.

Shakir, Evelyn. *Bint Arab: Arab and Arab American Women in the United States*. Westport, CT: Praeger, 1997.

Suleiman, Michael, ed. *Arabs in America: Building a New Future*. Philadelphia, PA: Temple University Press, 1999.

———. *Arabs in the Mind of America*. Brattleboro, VT: Amana Books, 1988.

Younis, Adele. *The Coming of the Arabic-Speaking People to the United States*. Philip Kayal, ed. New York: Center for Migration Studies, 1995.

CHAPTER 2

The Progressive Era and World War I: 1900 to 1920

IN THE EARLY 1900s, most Arabs living in the United States were immigrants. They had been born in the Ottoman Empire or other regions and had embarked on a six- to eight-week journey by boat, with an ultimate endpoint that was often little more than a hazy idea to them. Most traveled in third-class on board these ships, stuck below decks with minimal air and sunlight, and with little more than the name and contact information of a relative or family friend—someone who had already established a foothold in the United States, and who they hoped would house them and help them find work. These emigrants were mostly men, largely coming from rural areas in modern Lebanon, Syria, and Palestine, and with little formal education. The vast majority seem to have intended to stay in the United States only long enough to improve their family's economic position, or to establish themselves financially so they could return home to marry and re-settle in their country of origin.

By the turn of the century, a late-1800s downturn in the Ottoman rural economy had been sending a steady stream of Levantine Arabs to the United States and South America for nearly two decades. While estimates of the numbers of emigrants vary widely, scholar Kemal Karpat suggests that roughly 600,000 Arabs from Ottoman regions left for the Americas between 1860 and 1914—averaging approximately 11,000 per year. This meant that in some parts of the United States, there were sizable, fairly settled Arab communities, particularly in urban areas and factory towns. Most of these communities had formed through what scholars term the "chain migration" process: the establishment of a "chain" of migrants, each arriving there in search of a relative or friend who had already established himself or herself somewhere in the United States. In other parts of the country, Arab immigrants who peddled or settled in rural areas lived a more solitary life, getting together with their compatriots only during major holidays.

WORKING LIFE

While some Arab immigrants found jobs in textile and other factories in New England, and others moved to Michigan to work on the assembly lines of the Ford Motor Company, the vast majority of male Arab immigrants, as well as a fair number of females, worked as peddlers or traveling salesmen upon arrival in the United States. Some scholars estimate that one in three peddlers was a woman. Peddlers who proved successful often evolved into retail shop owners. The items that they sold ranged from "Holy Land" objects, such as vials of water said to be from the River Jordan, to pieces of ribbon, buttons, and other household goods—most aimed at women, whether for personal use or the household generally.

For newly arrived immigrants, peddling offered several advantages over factory or other service jobs. First, because peddlers generally worked under wholesalers who provided them with goods to sell, the job required very little start-up capital, which few immigrants had. Second, because peddlers were largely self-managing when it came to how quickly they sold the goods they carried, it enabled those with an entrepreneurial spirit and the willingness to pursue sales tirelessly to make far more money than if they worked in a factory or shop for an hourly wage. Third, peddling did not require an extensive command of English, and many peddlers found success in selling to other immigrant communities, such as German and Scandinavian farmers in the Midwest, for whom English was an equally foreign language.

The downsides to peddling were many—it was back-breaking work that involved long hours, and little wage stability. Peddlers, especially those just starting out or who earned too little to afford a horse to ride, generally walked from place to place, carrying their possessions and goods for sale. This was no light burden: a peddler walked with a suitcase or small trunk strapped to the back, hung another case around the neck, and carried a bag or knapsack filled with personal items and smaller goods in each hand or over the shoulder. The combined weight of all this baggage could range from 40 to 70 pounds. Yet to appear professional and respectable, peddlers often wore suits, which did little to make dusty, rainy, or snowy treks from one distant farmhouse to the next any easier. Moreover, peddlers depended on their clients for hot meals and a place to stay each night. In rural communities, taking in travelers was a fairly accepted practice—and peddlers often

Memoir of a High Plains Merchant

Mohammed (Ed) Aryain, the oldest son of a well-to-do farming family in central Syria that had fallen on hard times, emigrated to the United States in 1913, at age 15. He arrived to Ellis Island knowing no English and with nothing other than the name of another Syrian immigrant, a man named Mr. Tewell. Tewell had opened a successful notions and clothing wholesale operation in Rochester, Pennsylvania, and had agreed to look after Ed and give him a job. In this passage from Ed's memoir, *From Syria to Seminole: Memoir of a High Plains Merchant*, he had just been sent from Rochester to Beatrice, Nebraska, where he was to work as a door-to-door salesman with a team of other immigrant men. He had been in the country less than a month and spoke no English.

I arrived in Beatrice, Nebraska on the first day of July and was met at the depot by a group of Syrian men who also worked for Mr. Tewell. They told me that they had gathered together to celebrate the Fourth of July. This puzzled me until they explained what the holiday was, then I enjoyed it very much.

That evening while I was with these men and after we had become fairly well acquainted, one of them suggested I take for myself a new American name, as the name Mohammed would seem odd to the American people.

"What are the most common American names?" I asked, and they began suggesting "George," "Mack," "Joe," and "John." Then one of them said "Ed," and I liked this immediately, for it was short and sounded like the last part of my real name, so right then and there I decided I was Ed Aryain.

paid for their stay in bits of lace or other small items. But living the itinerant life meant that they had no fixed home, and bunking with America's immigrant farm communities meant that the home-cooked meals they were given featured unfamiliar foods and dishes that were very different from the *mezzeh* plates and grilled meats of the Levant. And the distance between farmsteads meant that a peddler could walk for miles without making a single sale—or arrive at dusk at the one house where the inhabitants refused to take in strangers.

As was true of most immigrants to the United States at the turn of the century, Arab immigrants from Ottoman territory were generally illiterate. However, a 1911 report by the U.S. Immigration Commission reported that "Syrian" immigrants (a general category often used in immigration records) reported higher skill levels than other immigrant groups, with 23 percent identifying themselves as practicing a skilled occupation and 20 percent identifying themselves as in trade, or what today might be called commerce

Among the small numbers of Arab immigrants working in agriculture were these Syrian children with a group of adults from Boston and Providence. They were photographed picking cranberries at the Maple Park Bog near East Wareham, Massachusetts, in September 1911.

or retail. The skills that immigrants claimed were most likely those related to farming, in keeping with their rural origins—but what is striking about Arab immigrants is how few took up farming in the United States. This may have been partly due to the differences in climate, crops, and farming techniques, but it also likely reflected the position in which newly arrived immigrants found themselves, as well as their economic goals. Peddling allowed them to earn cash money relatively quickly and, as noted above, with little capital outlay. Unlike a farm or any other enterprise requiring illiquid investment, it also allowed them to "cash out" quickly when or if they felt that they had earned enough to be able to return to the Arab world for a visit or for good.

On the other hand, peddling door-to-door was emotionally and physically taxing. Those who were successful often did begin putting down roots once they had saved enough money: investing in a wholesale or retail shop, and hiring newly arrived immigrants to do the peddling. Revenues from these shops provided a more comfortable living, while additional staffing by relatives or family friends from the same village allowed their owners to travel back to Lebanon, Palestine, or Syria for visits without being compelled to close or sell the store. In this way, immigrants joined America's middle and upper-middle classes.

RELIGIOUS LIFE

The vast majority of Arab immigrants in the United States at this time were Christian, belonging to one of several Orthodox or Catholic denominations. Muslim Arabs in the Ottoman Empire were more tightly policed by the government, and less able either to obtain permission to leave or to receive permission from their intended country to enter as an immigrant. Those Muslims who did migrate in search of work or other opportunities may have done so internally, within the empire's vast borders, or may have pretended to be Christian in order to emigrate. Once arrived in the United States, they may have practiced their faith quietly alone or gathered in small groups in someone's home; the first mosques started to appear in the Midwest in the 1910s, although they also served dual purposes as shops or offices. Other Muslims may have married Christians in the United States and raised their children in their spouse's faith. Yet while Christian Arabs may have found emigration to be an easier process, the different ritual practices, liturgical language, and theological tenets separating Orthodox and Catholic Arab Christians from the United States' overwhelmingly Protestant population meant that their faiths were considered almost as alien as Islam.

Despite their theological separation from the Episcopal, Lutheran, Methodist, Presbyterian, and other Protestant American communities, and their linguistic and ethnic separation from the country's emerging Irish and Italian Roman Catholic populations, religion played a central role in Christian Arab immigrants' individual and community lives. Towns and cities with any sizable settled immigrant population saw priests arriving from the Ottoman Empire starting in the 1890s—sent by bishops or even the patriarch at the request of immigrants anxious for the spiritual comfort and forms of worship of their particular denomination. Services were often held first in a private home, and then—once parishioners had committed funds—in a rented or purchased building. Land for a cemetery was often the next purchase, and Sunday

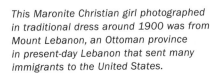

This Maronite Christian girl photographed in traditional dress around 1900 was from Mount Lebanon, an Ottoman province in present-day Lebanon that sent many immigrants to the United States.

school services and Arabic classes for U.S.-born children were an early priority as well. These purchases were particularly important as parishioners tended to live within walking distance of the church—which reinforced the tendency to cluster in neighborhoods or enclaves, limiting both their opportunities to live near non-Arabs, and to live near Arab immigrant communities of a different denomination.

While priests were solicited and churches were rented or built in order to preserve immigrants' spiritual link with their homeland, the process forced changes in tradition. Village churches were generally longstanding institutions; raising funds to establish a parish church was a new practice, as was the process of establishing the church's social pecking order. In the United States, the church's greatest patrons might be not the scions of elite families, but shop owners who had begun life as poor farmers and found success through peddling. Moreover, while chain migration meant that immigrant communities often included members of extended families or particular villages, the population of an Arab immigrant community such as Worcester, Massachusetts's Antiochian Orthodox community was more mixed than it would have been in Syria, Lebanon, or Palestine. As a result, church communities argued with one another over issues that ranged from the names that should be on the title deed, to the right to decide whether to keep a particular priest or send him back, as happened with some frequency.

CULTURAL LIFE: MUSIC AND THE PRESS

While religion served as one powerful means of knitting together Arab immigrant communities spiritually, music—through traveling artists and the trans-Atlantic circulation of wax records—and print culture, which included newspapers, journals, books, and magazines, served as similarly powerful cultural forces. Arab immigrants were able to listen to some of the same songs and instrumental pieces popular in the Levant thanks to the global presence of three early recording companies: Gramophone, a British company; Pathe, a French company; and Baidaphon, a Lebanese-owned company with a major office in Cairo. These firms recorded what they termed "native music" and sold the records not only throughout the Arab world, but also to Arab communities in North and South America—including the United States. Gramophones would have been a luxury for most immigrants, but the owners of cafes and restaurants appear to have seen both the records and their player as a business investment. During World War I, the flow of these records dried up almost entirely because of both production difficulties and shipping restrictions, but when the war ended, these firms were joined by several new companies, each eager to capitalize on wartime technological improvements and the hungry global market.

While the focus of recorded music in this period appears to have been on bringing music from the Arab world, Arab immigrant communities' print culture very quickly became a U.S.-based affair. By the early 1900s, several Arabic-language papers were published in the United States, most in New York. Most had religious and/or political affiliations: *Kawkub Amrika* (the Star of America) was an Orthodox Christian paper, while *Al Bayan* (the Message) was a Druze paper. In 1899 Naoum Mokarzel founded *Al Hoda*, which despite his personal identification as a Maronite Catholic, he presented as an unaffiliated paper aimed at all Arabic speakers. In keeping with his moderate views, *Al Hoda* encouraged readers to be loyal to both their Levantine homeland and their American home—and Mokarzel became a well-known figure in New York City thanks to his tireless advocacy of Arab immigrants and their acceptance within U.S. society.

A 1912 issue of Majallat al-Alam al-jadid al-nisaiyah *(The New World: A Ladies' Monthly Arabic Magazine), which was published in New York.*

Daily Arabic-language papers were relatively few; most published weekly or bi-monthly. Their issues included articles on U.S. affairs, but their primary appeal to readers was coverage of events and developments in the Arab world, which immigrants could not get in mainstream, English-language American papers. In addition to newspapers, the Arabic presses of New York and elsewhere published numerous literary and cultural journals, as well as a small number of books. By the 1910s works in English were appearing—starting with Ameen Rihani's 1911 novel *The Book of Khalid,* and including the early works of the famous Lebanese-American poet Kahlil Gibran. These and other writers' growing interest in English was a sign of the extent to which the Arab community had put down American roots; the children of the first and second generation of immigrants were coming of age, and for them English was increasingly the language of choice. While the heart of Arab-American literary activity remained in New York, the magazines, journals, and books of poetry—as well as newspapers—published there circulated throughout the United States, providing a cultural anchor that connected immigrants first with their homeland, and subsequently with the evolving culture of their American home.

ARAB-AMERICAN URBAN COMMUNITIES: NEW YORK

The vast majority of Arab immigrants entered the United States through New York's Ellis Island. However, because there were almost no U.S. entry restrictions for Mexican citizens at the time, those Arabs who were unable to obtain a visa could enter through Mexico if they stayed there long enough to obtain residency or could successfully pass as Mexican when crossing the border. As a result, New York was widely seen as the gateway to the United States—and in some cases synonymous with it. While Arab immigrant communities could be found throughout New York State, the biggest and most

Immigrants disembarking from a ferry at Ellis Island in the early 20th century. New York was both the main entry point for Arab immigrants and home to a vital Arab community.

visible concentration was in New York City—in the area near Washington Street known as Little Syria. Little Syria offered banks, restaurants, shops selling goods and foods familiar to Arab immigrants, and jobs to newly arrived immigrants who were hired as peddlers for the area's wholesalers. Most importantly, it provided the foundation of a thriving ethnic community.

What this meant was that newly arrived immigrants found in New York others who spoke Arabic, shared their culture, and provided both an emotional cushion and the practical network to help them through the often dislocating process of arriving in a completely foreign country. Since so many immigrants came from rural backgrounds, this also helped them with the equally discombobulating experience of navigating the very large, urban spaces of New York City. While most immigrants did not remain in New York, the city's role as a clearinghouse and as a symbol of the rich vibrancy of urban immigrant life made it a reference for immigrants around the country, as well as for friends and family back in the Levant.

ARAB-AMERICAN RURAL COMMUNITIES: OKLAHOMA

Oklahoma's Arab communities developed from the numerous peddlers who began traveling around the state, selling goods to the families of farmers and

Little Syria, New York
"The Quiet Syrian Colony"

The cultural, ethnic, and linguistic diversity of New York's populations was an aspect of the city that its leading institutions celebrated, even when framing them as "foreign" to what they saw as its British- or at least northwestern European–inflected "American" core identity. This identity is also expressed through food: "Americans" seem to have been understood to prefer a blander, simpler diet.

The following excerpt is taken from a long *New York Times* article from August 28, 1898, that featured capsule descriptions of New York's ethnic enclaves. The article was accompanied by photos of "typical" inhabitants, both as head-shots, and set in the broader context of the buildings and sights described as characteristic of the neighborhood.

In the southwest corner of New York, directly over against the vast, feverish money mart of this city of Mammon, one may find the quiet Syrian colony. It differs much from other foreign quarters in New York. It is fairly clean. There is nothing forbidding in the aspect of the people or their places of business. There are women and children to add their cheery presence. The homes are clean and inviting, and the stores, where Turkish rugs, laces, perfumes, and tobacco are sold, display evidences of prosperity.

The Syrians in New York [City] number about 2,000 and occupy Washington Street and the west side cross streets from Greenwich to Battery Park. One of the features of the place is the Turkish restaurants. A meal at one of these is an ordeal few Americans care to undergo. While everything is scrupulously clean, the dishes are all seasoned so highly and are so rich in oils and fats that our plain American digestive apparatus loudly rebels against them. Then, when the mysterious hubble-bubble [the nargileh, or water-pipe], with its water bottle, hose, and bulb, is brought and the dark, coarse tobacco lighted, it requires a mighty knight ... to stand this supreme test [since smoking tobacco in this form was much stronger than smoking a cigarette or a pipe]. Native men, women, and children all smoke the hubble-bubble.

... Another feature of the Syrian quarter is that the famous Turkish dancers [i.e., "belly" dancers] who first startled the Midway, and who have now become a common feature of Coney Island and other resorts are to be found there. The Syrian papers and the better class of people are doing their utmost to suppress this infamy.

Two Syrian priests minister to the religious needs of the colony, and on public festival days the costumes of the people are picturesque in the extreme.

ranchers starting in the mid 1890s. Their presence is reflected in the peddler figure in the musical *Oklahoma!*, who was described as a "Persian" in the Rodgers and Hammerstein musical, and as a Syrian immigrant in the Lynn Riggs play and Broadway hit *Green Grow the Lilacs*, on which the musical version was based. While sizable communities grew up in Oklahoma City and Tulsa, many immigrants first found jobs selling door-to-door in smaller towns where they were often some of the only Arabic speakers. Their life was a solitary one, and much of their time was spent either alone in rooming houses or—while on the road—with strangers who housed them for a night or two. Those who did not peddle or open a retail store took up farming or entered the oil business.

RACE ISSUES: "NOT QUITE WHITE"

Perhaps the greatest challenge faced by immigrants in small towns or midsized cities—like those in Oklahoma, where they were visible, but small minorities—was racism. With racial identity in the United States conceived almost exclusively in terms of white and black—and with clear privileges accruing to those classified as white and clear discrimination heaped upon those classified as black—determining the race of Arab immigrants, along with Irish, Italian, Spanish, and other southern Europeans, was seen as critical to determining their eligibility for U.S. citizenship. The "teeming masses"

Syrian children playing on the street in New York City in the early 20th century. The New York Times *estimated there were 2,000 Syrians in the city's Little Syria neighborhood in 1898.*

"A Brilliantly Picturesque Figure"

In the late 1800s and into the 1900s, the *New York Times* ran a weekly column that reported on the social and charitable activities of "society," or upper- and upper-middle-class women. This excerpt from January 27, 1895, records the reaction of such women to the visit of an affluent Syrian woman:

At the regular Thursday morning meeting of the Ladies' Club, 28 East Twenty-second Street, last Thursday, Mme. Hanna Korany gave the members an interesting account of the manner of life of Syrian women. Mme. Korany was a brilliantly picturesque figure in her Oriental robes of bright red and yellow, with gold-embroidered turban and white veil.

She astonished most of the club members and guests by telling them that her compatriots, the Syrian women, dressed almost entirely according to the French fashions, which reach Syria quite as soon as they do this country.

Her countrywomen not only wear the European styles, Mme. Korany said, but they wear them with better taste than either the European or American women. The elder women always wear the most elegant material, leaving the pretty but less expensive goods for the young girls or young married women. The older women wear modified forms of all fashions. If large sleeves are in vogue, the older matrons adopt them in a less exaggerated degree.

The women of the South and East, Mme. Korany informed her listeners, she believed to be much more beautiful than the women of colder climates, where a devoted adherence is given to social and other duties ... About fifty persons were present at the meeting.

of humanity who began pouring through Ellis Island after its 1892 opening were allowed to enter the United States, but not all were welcome as citizens—including Arabs. Starting in 1906, a small but steady number of Arab immigrants from the Levant began to turn to the U.S. court system to argue that they were white, and hence deserved citizenship. They used a number of different arguments: their long history of civilization, their identity as Semites, their Christian religion, and various personal qualifications. Judges on the other hand tended to see whiteness as determined by skin color and western European ancestry.

After nearly a decade of various court cases, *Dow v. United States*, settled in late 1915, established a largely definitive legal precedent in favor of the idea that Levantine Arabs, particularly Christian Arabs, were white and thus eligible for U.S. citizenship. However, socially and in most contexts, Lebanese, Palestinians,

Syrians, and other Arabs were treated as "not quite white": as racially inferior to Americans of northern and western European origin. They faced informal discrimination in business, education, and government dealings, and during times of tension in some towns became victims of physical attacks.

IDENTITY ISSUES: "SA'IH" AND "MAHJAR"

As previously noted, establishing lifelong residency or settling permanently in the United States was not the goal of most Arab immigrants. While statistical estimates vary, scholars agree that approximately one-third of all Arab immigrants to the Americas, including the United States, returned to their homeland. Some re-emigrated within a few years, but overall, roughly one-quarter of all Arab immigrants seem to have returned permanently to their native land. Even for those who stayed, identifying as "American" may have been relatively uncommon; instead they continued to identify as Ottomans, Lebanese, Syrians, or Palestinians living abroad, as well as identifying with their natal villages.

Some of this can be seen from the terms that Arab immigrants used to describe themselves. For example, in the early 1900s Abdul Massih Haddad, known as Albert in the United States, started a bi-monthly New York–based newspaper called *As-Sayeh*. The word *sayeh* (sa'iH) means "tourist" in contemporary Arabic, but in this context it meant "traveler" or "sojourner"—in other words, it described someone on a journey far from home who was intending to return. Similarly, immigrants generally described themselves as living in the *mahjar*—living abroad. Over time, the term took on a life of its own, referring collectively to the Arab diaspora, and particularly that of the Americas. But describing oneself as "living abroad" or defining oneself as part of a "diaspora"—even after 20 years or more of living in the United States—was a clear indication that for these immigrants, taking on "American" identity was not a primary goal.

IDENTITY ISSUES: NAME CHANGES

Changing one's name upon entry to the United States has historically been part of many immigrants' stories, due in large part to the difficulty that immigration authorities and others had in correctly pronouncing and spelling unfamiliar names. Officials recording arrivals at Ellis Island sometimes wrote new arrivals' names as spelled on the manifests of the European ships in which they arrived; sometimes they took names down directly, spelling them either phonetically or approximating them with names more familiar to English-speaking ears. For many Arab immigrants, the changes to their first and last names seem to have come at different moments, or to have served different purposes.

First name changes may have been at once more practical and more poignant, because changing one's first name means giving up the name cho-

Immigrants at Ellis Island in 1902 waiting to have their papers examined by immigration officials. Many immigrant families altered their surnames either on arrival or after settling in the United States.

sen by one's parents and used by family and close friends. Yet given that Arab immigration in this period was primarily driven by economic interests, changing one's first name seems to have been seen as a critical step to getting, holding, and achieving success in a job. For those who began peddling, working in factories with non-Arab coworkers and foremen, or working in shops where they were likely to encounter non-Arab employers and customers, having a first name that was both familiar and easy to pronounce may have been seen as a professional necessity. In general, the first names that immigrants took were either English translations of their Arabic names—for example, "Boutros" might have become "Peter"—or English names that began with the same letter as their Arabic name. In some cases, immigrants seem to have chosen names based simply on whether they liked the sound of them.

The use of last names, in the sense of a constant term transferred from generation to generation on the father's side, was a relatively late development in the Arabic-speaking world and the Ottoman Empire more broadly. What emerged as last names were terms generally taken from the adjective called a *nisba*, or *laqab* in Arabic, especially in Lebanon and Syria, that was historically used to identify an individual person by occupation, geographic origin, or—for elite figures—well-known tribal families or clans.

Although by the early 1900s last names were still a somewhat nascent concept, they accumulated meaning for their bearers relatively quickly, as evidenced by the way that Arab immigrants did not abandon them entirely upon arrival. In some cases they chose an English translation: for example, "Haddad" might have become "Smith." In other cases, they seem to have tried to preserve some visual or phonetic similarity, despite the orthographic and ethnic changes wrought by immigration officials, rather than adopting new names entirely. For example, "Faris" became "Ferris," "Dagher" became "Decker," and "Barakat" became "Berrick"—all changes that stripped away the overtly Arabic aspects of these last names (including their meaning) while preserving several key structural elements: initial sound, overall consonant or vowel flow, and/or number of syllables. Since many immigrants were illiterate—and even those literate in Arabic were unlikely to read Roman script—some name changes may have been made by officials before the immigrants even realized it.

In addition to the economic motives and the role of immigration authorities, there are several reasons why newly arrived immigrants did not keep their original names, or did not take them back once more firmly established in the United States. Names, like language, signaled belonging to a culture, if not a nation, and were a way to fit in. New or altered names were also a way of protecting themselves from rejection, abuse, and unwelcome curiosity.

The exceptions to this process were few, but striking. Immigrants who settled in New York, for example, were much less likely to change either their first or last names: the Arab community in New York City was large enough, and the city's overall population diverse enough, that having an Arabic name was not necessarily the economic disadvantage that it might have been in Wisconsin, Texas, or Oregon.

RELATIONS WITH THE OTTOMAN EMPIRE

While many immigrants grew accustomed over time to the idea that the United States would be their permanent home, most still seem to have hoped to return to their native land to visit family members and often (at least for the men) in hopes of finding a local bride. Some appear to have traveled back on U.S. passports. Those who returned as Ottoman citizens, however, faced the question of how warmly the government would receive them.

By the late 1800s, the Ottoman government—with upper-level bureaucrats who were often well-educated, progressive reformers rather than the decadent despots of European stereotype—was facing economic, political, and social pressures because of the increasing interference of European governments and the Ottomans' own military losses, mostly to Russia. As a result the government tried to minimize emigration by preventing citizens, especially Muslim citizens, from leaving. It feared that their loss would deprive the empire of needed human resources, and that Ottoman citizens

A 1920 photograph of a mosque overlooking a number of small villages in Mount Lebanon province. Emigrants from this region are estimated to have sent back remittances accounting for 41 percent of its economy by the 1910s.

abroad might fall into debt or disrepute, further denigrating the empire's image in European eyes.

But Ottoman subjects abroad were also lucrative sources of government revenue. First, at the moment of emigration, through the fees it charged for citizens needing passports, birth certificates, and other official documents; for arranging medical exams, providing official translators for applications and interviews with U.S. and South American consulates; and—less officially—for bribes paid to individual officials when the results of a medical exam were negative, or an applicant was deemed too young to emigrate alone.

Second, through remittances: money sent via wire transfer or in the care of traveling friends. In keeping with the economic focus of Ottoman subjects' migration, most emigrants sent a portion of their earnings home on a regular basis to aid parents, siblings, and sometimes wives and children in financial need. By the 1910s, scholars estimate that 41 percent of the economy of Mount Lebanon, an Ottoman province in today's Lebanon and a major source of migrants, came from remittances. As a result most emigrants returning to the Ottoman Empire to visit or resettle seem to have been able to do so with no trouble.

THE CHALLENGE OF RETURN

Those emigrants who returned to their homeland with the intent of resettling permanently in their native village often found that coming home was a greater challenge than they anticipated. First, they faced the pressure of the great expectations that family, friends, and neighbors had for them. As returnees from America, they were expected to be wealthy and to dispense that wealth generously. Those who had not found financial success in the United States appear to have tried hard to disguise this fact on visits home, to delay visits in hopes of achieving success, or to avoid returning entirely. An emigrant's financial success in "Amerka" was shown by his or her possessions: gold watches for men, fur coats for women, and large cuckoo clocks as gifts for family members.

Second and perhaps more importantly, emigrants returning home after several years abroad in the United States found that both they and their homes—including their families—had changed. Coming home was not always a smooth process. Most emigrants left as young men, spending their formative years far from their natal families, and in a working environment that required them to develop a much higher degree of self-reliance. They returned as adults with years of work and personal experiences that differed substantially from those of family and friends back home. They also came back changed by their immersion in American culture: they had grown accustomed to a different pace of life, to new foods and manners of eating, to alternate forms of interaction between family and friends, and to the very different level of 'creature comforts'—such as electricity—that the United States offered. When they returned, they found that home suddenly looked a bit foreign, with the dirt roads, rough clothing, and lack of running water and electricity that characterized such villages.

This 1917 poster promoted an American campaign to assist survivors of World War I in Syria and other Near Eastern countries.

While few Arab immigrants consciously decided to adopt American behaviors, over time their ideas of how to relate to family and friends evolved into a hybrid of Arab and American culture as city-driven, American concepts of middle-class life began to influence them. Their views on husband-wife and parent-child relations were inflected by American middle-class notions about families in which the husband and father worked at a job that did not require physical labor, the wife "made a home," and the children focused on school and play. Their notion of an appropriate housing layout including distinct sleeping, living, and eating rooms, in which parents and children slept in separate rooms. During mealtimes, they preferred to eat in straight-backed chairs, using full sets of cutlery. All of this made a permanent return to an immigrant's natal village difficult—and the difficulty increased the longer the immigrant remained in the United States.

CONCLUSION

World War I broke out in Europe as a combination of racist and nativist sentiments led toward the culmination of Arab immigrant efforts to obtain the right to American citizenship through the court system. Although the Ottoman Empire entered the war on the side of Germany and the Triple Alliance, the wave of anti-German feeling that swept parts of the United States does not appear to have affected Arab immigrants to the same degree. The war curtailed the easy transit of mail and goods between the United States and the Ottoman Empire, leaving immigrants unable to send letters or money to family back in the Levant for several years. The severe political dislocations, brutal war years, and severe famines that struck Lebanon and Syria in particular meant that when the war ended, the flow of Arab immigrants—and, perhaps more importantly, the increase in their desire to leave—increased.

ANDREA STANTON
NEW YORK UNIVERSITY

Further Reading

Akarli, Engin. "Ottoman Attitudes towards Lebanese Emigration, 1885–1910," in Albert Hourani and Nadim Shehadi, eds. *The Lebanese in the World: A Century of Emigration.* London: IB Tauris, 1992.

Aryain, Ed, and J'Nell Pate. *From Syria to Seminole: Memoir of a High Plains Merchant.* Lubbock, TX: Texas Tech University Press, 2006.

Elias, Leila Salloum. "The Impact of the Sinking of the *Titanic* on the New York Syrian Community of 1912: The Syrians Respond," *Arab Studies Quarterly,* Vol. 27, 2005.

Ellis, Raff. *Kisses from a Distance.* Seattle, WA: Cune Press, 2007.

Gabbert, Ann. "El Paso, A Sight for Sore Eyes: Medical and Legal Aspects of Syrian Immigration, 1906–1907," *The Historian,* Vol. 65, No. 1, October 2002.

Gualtieri, Sarah. "Becoming 'White': Race, Religion and the Foundations of Syrian/Lebanese Ethnicity in the United States," *Journal of American Ethnic History,* summer 2001.

———. "Gendering the Chain Migration Thesis: Women and Syrian Transatlantic Migration, 1878–1924," *Comparative Studies of South Asia, Africa and the Middle East,* Vol. 24, No. 1, 2004.

Haddad, Yvonne Yazbeck. *Not Quite American? The Shaping of Arab and Muslim Identity in the United States.* Waco, TX: Baylor University Press, 2004.

Kayyali, Randa. *The Arab Americans.* Westport, CT: Greenwood Press, 2005.

Khater, Akram. *Inventing Home: Emigration, Gender, and the Middle Class in Lebanon, 1870–1920.* Berkeley, CA: University of California Press, 2001.

Saliba, Najib. *Emigration from Syria and the Syrian-Lebanese Community of Worcester, MA.* Ligonier, PA: Antakya Press, 1992.

Shakir, Evelyn. *Remember Me to Lebanon: Stories of Lebanese Women in America.* Syracuse, NY: Syracuse University Press, 2007.

Suleiman, Michael, ed. *Arabs in America.* Philadelphia, PA: Temple University Press, 1999.

———. "The Mokarzels' Contributions to the Arabic-Speaking Community in the United States," *Arab Studies Quarterly*, spring 1999.

CHAPTER 3

The Roaring Twenties and Great Depression: 1920 to 1939

WORLD WAR I was both a watershed in the history of the modern Middle East, and a major catalyst in the history of Arab Americans. In the Middle East, the post–World War I era saw the dismantling of the Ottoman Empire and the creation of a series of new colonial entities under the rule of the British and French, called Mandates, as well as the sovereign states of the Gulf and Arabian peninsulas. As imperial masters over these lands for the next two to three decades, the British and French used brutal force and social disruption as methods of rule to create what were to become the new Arab states of the region: Lebanon, Syria, Iraq, and Transjordan (Jordan). These new colonies were in addition to the previously held colonies of Egypt (by Britain); Tunisia, Algeria, and Morocco (by France); and Libya (by Italy). In the case of Palestine, the British fostered the Jewish nationalist movement, Zionism, in a process of state-creation that eventually led to the formation of Israel in 1948.

These new political realities in the region, with all their upheavals, dislocations, and political disenfranchisement, led to an increase in immigration to the Americas, in particular to the United States. Furthermore, those Arab Americans who were born in or had been living in the United States for decades were deeply affected by the plight of their former communities, families, and friends in their lands of origin. The problems of the region, as well as the new ideologies, movements, and social changes that emerged out

A British landing party hauls a field gun and ammunition wagon from their ship into the desert in the Persian Gulf region between 1910 and 1920. British and French involvement in the region exacerbated poor conditions for local populations and led to increased emigration.

of the postwar environment influenced the political and cultural activities of Arab Americans, and caused some to reassess their definitions of identity and social loyalties.

Many of the trends that began in the Arab-American communities in the 1920s continued into the 1930s. There was still a limit on Arab immigration because of the quotas set by the Immigration Act of 1924 (the Johnson-Reed Act). Arab Americans, especially intellectuals, paid increasing attention to the deteriorating situation for Palestinians in British Mandate Palestine. Arab Americans were still primarily loyal to their sectarian and familial identities, but like in the 1920s, emerging voices and debates promoted new nationalistic ideologies that were reconfiguring identity in the Middle East as they would come to change Arab Americans. An example of the growing role of nationalist ideology was the more frequent use of the term "Lebanese" instead of "Syrian" for self-identification by Arab Americans whose origins were from Mount Lebanon.

Like in earlier decades, Arab Americans continued to be mainly clustered in or around urban centers, with industrial cities such as Detroit rivaling New York in the size of its Arab-American community. However, despite the continuity of all these trends from the 1920s, the Depression slowed the pace of immigration and redirected these immigrants to new locations in the United States that had not yet experienced a large influx of Arab Americans. The Depression also affected Arab Americans—as it affected all those who lived in the United States—by limiting the availability of funds for communal, religious, cultural, and political activities and associations. Thus, while many of the same organizations and newspapers that were founded in earlier decades continued to operate in the 1930s, fewer new ones were formed, and some of the older ones closed down.

IMMIGRATION AND SETTLEMENT PATTERNS IN THE 1920s

Up to the 1920s, Arab immigration was pioneered by single males, with around 75 percent between the ages of 15 and 45. Once they established themselves, family and friends came to join them. However, the Arab immigration of the 1920s was characterized by a larger percentage of women than men coming to the United States. By the end of what most historians consider the first wave of Arab immigrants (roughly starting in the 1880s and continuing until the period during and/or immediately after World War I), there were approximately 200,000 Arabs in the United States, though it is impossible to state this with exactitude. For the four years prior to World War I, the total number of Arab immigrants was just over 29,000, but then slowed down to a trickle (1,767 people in 1915 and then ranging from 210 to 976 for the next four years) due to war conditions. Afterward, the period between the end of World War I and 1924 saw a surge of Arab immigrants, numbering approximately 12,228. The new immigration laws in 1924 greatly limited the numbers of Arabs coming in from that year onward. Yearly quotas for each region of the world meant that on average, in the latter part of the 1920s, the number of Arabs coming in to the United States was in the hundreds per year.

Based on the immigration records, the point of origin for the largest percentage of these immigrants was "Syria" (today's Syria is a much diminished remnant of what should more properly be called "Greater Syria," which at the time comprised the Mount Lebanon area, the region of Palestine, parts of modern day Iraq and Turkey, as well as today's Syria). Depending on the year, they usually made up 70–80 percent of the total number of immigrants. A smaller percentage was made up of Egyptians, followed by immigrants from Iraq. Finally, much smaller waves of Arab immigrants came from North Africa (today's Morocco, Algeria, Tunisia, and Libya) and the Arabian Peninsula (and consistently, of this latter group, the overwhelming majority came from Yemen). The immigrants were typically poor, from rural

A row of shops on Monroe Avenue in Detroit in 1928. Store ownership remained an avenue for advancement for Arab peddlers in the 1920s.

peasant backgrounds, though some had craft and industrial skills. There was a relatively high degree of illiteracy among immigrants in the earlier part of the 20th century, perhaps as high as 40 percent, but by the 1920s only about 21 percent of these immigrants were illiterate.

The years from 1918 to 1922 saw a significant wave of Muslim Arabs (primarily from Mount Lebanon but also Yemen) come to Michigan to work in the auto industry: first Highland Park, then Dearborn, in order to work at the Ford Motor Company factories. Urban areas, especially along the East Coast of the United States, saw the highest concentrations of Arab communities. By 1930, the combined total of "Syrians" living in Manhattan and Brooklyn in New York City was 7,631, with many smaller communities clustered around the city and in its suburbs. Detroit's "Syrian" population had been steadily rising, reaching 5,520 in 1930, while Boston's community was shrinking from its high of roughly 3,000.

IMMIGRATION AND SETTLEMENT PATTERNS IN THE 1930s

The most noticeable issue for the Arab-American community in the 1930s was the very small influx of more Arabs from abroad. As immigration quotas were still in effect since 1924, the total number of Arab immigrants coming to the

The Ford Motor Company in Detroit employed so many immigrants in the early 20th century that it conducted its own English classes. These foreign-born workers were attending a Ford Training Services English class sometime between 1909 and 1932.

An aerial view of the Dodge auto plant in 1930 surrounded by clusters of worker housing in the community of Hamtramck, Michigan. Hamtramck was dominated by Poles for much of the 20th century, but a small Arab community later drew many new Arab immigrants to the area.

United States in the 1930s was approximately 1,500. This limitation on Arab immigrants was not only a demographic issue, but also affected communal, social, and religious facets of Arab-American communities. For example, it was harder for Arabs to find Arab spouses, thus encouraging exogamy (marrying outside one's community, tribe, or clan). The various sectarian communities, especially the very small ones such as the Chaldeans, often found it hard to maintain viable congregations; in tandem with a lack of clergy, these factors combined meant the rapid decimation of religious practice and traditions.

Furthermore, the depressed situation in the United States and lack of jobs caused many Arab immigrants to either move on to another location (South America) or return home, with some historians suggesting this was as high as 60 percent of the Arab immigrants throughout the 1930s. Also, among the comparatively large numbers of Arab immigrants that went to Detroit in the 1930s looking for work in the auto industry, some found the situation there difficult and then moved to the southern United States and engaged in farm work. Since Arab Americans, like everybody in the United States, were desperately seeking work, they were more likely to move to new locations with no, or very small, pre-existing Arab communities. This process distributed Arab Americans in ever-widening waves throughout the country, but also diluted the size of communities and further led to decimation of communal and cultural strength. Regardless, by the end of the decade in 1940, the estimated total of Arab Americans was around 800,000.

SECTARIAN IDENTITY AND QUESTIONS OF ASSIMILATION

The various Arab communities in the United States should not be thought of as a monolithic entity, as there were various social and cultural differences among Arabs, with the most important distinguishing characteristic being sectarian. The overwhelming majority of Arab immigrants to the United States were Christian, or rather, so-called Eastern Christians. Followers of "eastern-rite" churches, their religious services were conducted in Arabic, Syriac, or Chaldean-Aramaic and these sects included: Melkite, Maronite, Orthodox, and smaller numbers of Assyrian, Aramean, Chaldean, and Coptic. It is estimated that by 1924 there were 75 churches of the first three sects, clustered in communities in 28 states, mainly located on the East Coast.

Because some of the smaller sects were unable to establish religious institutions (no priests or not a large enough community) this meant either the community would await itinerant priests, or they might attend the services of other churches. In the latter case, members of some of the Eastern Christian sects, as either Eastern Catholic or Eastern Orthodox, would attend the services of Roman Catholic or Greek Orthodox churches, respectively. This would lead to ritual and linguistic loss; for example, Maronites attending Catholic churches would have to accept the Latin language and ritual. Furthermore, for some Arabs, adapting to their situation might mean joining the much larger and better-funded Roman Catholic and Protestant churches, thus causing a steady stream of intersectarian conversions. Some Arab Americans also saw conversion to "mainstream" Christian sects as part of the Americanization process. This issue of loss of adherence to the Eastern Christian sects (and their particular rites) began to become a debating point in the 1930s.

Whereas for previous decades and earlier Arab immigrant waves, assimilation into mainstream society was a goal, the awakening of Arab nationalist sentiments in the Middle East and the new post–World War I political order in the region affected those Arabs already in the United States. Perhaps the core of the debate in the 1930s was the role of religion, and given that the overwhelming majority of the immigrants were Christian, this debate had to do with the perceived loss of heritage when Arabs embraced American Protestantism, or to a lesser degree, Roman Catholicism. For those Arab-American intellectuals at the forefront of this debate, there was the double threat of the reduction of the size of the Eastern Christian communities—Greek Orthodox, Maronite, Melkite, Assyrian, Aramean, Chaldean, Coptic—as well as the belief that in converting to "mainstream" American Christian sects (Protestantism or Roman Catholicism), these Arab Americans lost the single most important link to their cultural heritage and family back in their coun-

Bishop (St.) Raphael of Brooklyn (left), who was the head of the Syrian Greek Orthodox Catholic Mission in North America, meeting with Archbishop Platon (center), the head of the Russian Orthodox church in North America, and Bishop Alexander of Alaska at St. Tikhon's Monastery in South Canaan, Pennsylvania, in an American news service photograph from the early 1900s.

try of origin. To combat the possibility of conversion, some Eastern Christian churches attempted to Americanize certain aspects of their ritual activities. On the other hand, as scholar Philip Kayal has noted, "By modifying their rites and the symbols of their 'corporate identity' so as to make them more American, the Syrians unwittingly destroyed the basis for their own community life." As seen in earlier decades, despite this debate and attempts to stem the tide of conversion, a steady stream of Arab Americans were converting and diluting the communal strength and existence of the Eastern Christian churches.

Muslim Arabs were found in the same cities as other significant Arab communities, yet they dealt with many more social obstacles in practicing their faith. While the first record of Muslims organizing for communal prayer was in a private home in Ross, North Dakota in 1900, they were only able to build a mosque there in 1920; yet they became so integrated that they intermarried with Christians, adopted Christian names, and the mosque was closed by 1948. Michigan saw the establishment of two Islamic institutions at this time, one in Highland Park in 1919, and the other in the Detroit-Dearborn area in 1922. In 1924 a Young Men's Muslim Association (YMMA) for Arab Muslims

Arabic Newspapers

The Arab-American communities in the 1920s enjoyed a decent diversity of Arabic-language newspapers. Due to the fact that very few copies of the newspapers (especially the smaller ones) have survived, what follows is a discussion of the most important, largest, or longest-lived. The earliest Arabic-language newspapers printed in the United States set the trend that was to distinguish the Arabic press for quite some time: they were in New York City and had sectarian affiliations. Newspapers established in the early 20th century included *al-Sa'ih* ("The Traveler," 1912–57), which was founded by Orthodox 'Abd al-Masih Haddad. Serving the Druze community in the Detroit area was *al-Bayan* ("The News") which was founded by Sulayman Budur in 1910 and lasted until 1960, incorporating *al-Sa'ih* in 1957. After the literary magazine *al-Funun* folded in 1918, it was a decade later when Abu Madi founded *al-Samir*, which lasted from 1929 to 1957. There were numerous short-lived papers and many were closely affiliated with particular Arab literati or certain families; for example, between the years 1898 and 1954, members of the Mukarzil family founded seven newspapers.

These papers were both a source of local news, as well as a means to remain connected with the community and events back in the Arab world. Not only were they sectarian in affiliation, but they also generally maintained certain political positions. For example, the early newspaper *Kawkub Amrika* expressed editorial support of the Ottoman government, whereas other papers such as *al-Ayam* ("the Days") and *al-Mushir* ("the Advisor") took generally hostile positions against Ottoman rule. With the destruction of Ottoman rule over Arab lands during World War I and the subsequent British- and French-directed colonial projects in the region, these papers were an active forum debating the relative merits of supporting or rejecting the new colonial masters.

Due to ideological and sectarian loyalties, it was often the case that these debates were heated and continually revealed the splintered nature of the Arab American communities. For example, the editor of *al-Huda*, the Maronite Na'um Mukarzil, used his paper as a platform to argue for the preference of adopting the term "Lebanese" instead of "Syrian" as a marker of identity.

The various Arab communities in the 1930s continued to be served by the various pre-existing newspapers, but with the increase in size of many Arab-American communities, a number of new newspapers were founded in the 1930s. These included the Chaldean newspaper *al-Islah* ("the Reform") in New York, founded in 1933 by an Iraqi, Father al-Funus Shurayz. The year 1940 saw the foundation of *al-Hayah* ("Life") in the Detroit area by a Sunni Muslim imam, Husayn Khuroub, though this was later reorganized as *al-Risalah al-Arabaiyah-al-Amrikiyah* ("the Arab-American Message") in 1948.

was established in Brooklyn, which tried to meet the needs of the Muslim community there. But until the larger numbers of Muslims came in the late 1940s, there were very few mosques built in the country.

Some estimates of the Muslim-Arab population in the 1930s put it around 25,000, with the largest communities being in Detroit (10,000), New York (5,000), Cleveland (2,000), and other East Coast locations. At that time, as now, the Muslim-Arab population was far outnumbered by other Muslim Americans (immigrants from Asia and African Americans). Muslim Arabs, even more than Christian Arabs, found it difficult to maintain strong outward devotion to the faith in such a predominantly Christian society, especially after the Immigration Act of 1924 and the more xenophobic sociopolitical currents in the United States of the 1920s that produced the Immigration Act. It has been claimed that the Muslim-Arab community in the 1920s soon became assimilated, sometimes with the loss of traditional Islamic practices. Single Muslim-Arab men found it difficult to find Muslim spouses. Furthermore, the difficulties associated with building mosques and getting trained Muslim clergy to come and serve the communities in the United States also proved detrimental.

It should be noted that there was also a significant number of what were called "Syrian Jews" who came to the United States in the first quarter of the 20th century. They primarily came from Aleppo and Damascus (in present-day Syria) and settled mostly in the New York and New Jersey area. Like other immigrants from the region at that time, they were identified as Syrian or

The struggling congregation of St. Mary's Syrian Orthodox Church (shown above in 1988) lost the Johnstown, Pennsylvania, building during the Depression but was able to repurchase it in 1941. They worshipped there until the early 1970s, when a Serbian Orthodox group took it over.

The Mahjar Writers

The most famous Arab-American cultural society of the early 20th century was the celebrated literary society al-Rabitah al-Qalamiyah, which means "the Pen Bond." This society was based in New York City and evolved in two phases: the first was in 1916 with nine members, including Kahlil Gibran (1883–1931), Ameen Rihani (1876–1940), Amin Mushriq (1894–1938), Nasib Aridah (1887–1946), Abdal-Masih Haddad (1881–1950), and William Catzeflis. They were hoping to encourage a revival of Arabic language and literature, which they felt had declined while the Arabs were under Ottoman rule, while at the same time introducing new literary forms and themes that they had absorbed during their lives in the United States. For example, this meant the introduction of free verse into Arabic poetry.

They also saw themselves as promoters of reform, modernism, and social activism. They were quite concerned about the destruction and famine in their homeland, Greater Syria, during World War I, and then in the post–World War I period they focused their attention on British and French policies in their Arab colonies. They published their writings, which included poetry, essays, and journalistic work, in the Arabic newspapers *al-Funun* (which means "the Arts" and was published in New York City 1913–18) and *al-Sa'ih* ("the Traveler"). The society was reincarnated in 1920 and lasted until 1931, including some of the earlier members, plus more prominent roles for men like Mikhail Naimy, whereas Ameen Rihani left the society and began to travel the Middle East in order to pursue a new political activist agenda in his writing. Over time, other prominent Arab writers in the Arab world began to affiliate or become "correspondents" of the society, such as the famous woman Palestinian-Lebanese writer May Ziyadah (or Ziade) (1886–1941).

As this group of Arab-American intellectuals became known in the Arab world (as their works were published in the Arab press), they were called the "Mahjar writers," (or "Mahjar poets") meaning writers of the "emigration," or "emigrant writers." Over time their poetic innovations began to have some influence on poetry written in the Arab world, and their political and intellectual activism, which was underscored by their broad international and cross-cultural experiences, enabled them to make an impact on the political and cultural debates of their day.

Levantine, and based on personal, cultural, and social criteria they could be considered Arab Americans. Over later decades, questions of identity were mixed with politics, especially in light of the strength of Zionist ideology in Jewish communities, and thus most did not embrace the label of Arab Jews; many of these Syrian Jews primarily emphasized the term Sephardic Jews (though Mizrahi Jew is becoming a more popular term among those Middle Eastern Jews who now live in Israel).

SOCIAL ACTIVISM AND PROFESSIONAL ORGANIZATIONS

The Arab-American community in the 1920s continued to be served by a variety of associations that had been formed in earlier years. Usually these associations were very local in concern and activities, but given the size of the Arab community in New York City, this city had larger and more notable groups (of which there are records). The political upheavals and influence of various ideological and political loyalties in the post–World War I period were catalytic for the Arab-American community, and inspired the formation of a plethora of new sociopolitical organizations. While some organizations seemed to be primarily sectarian in their membership or interests, many others showed a diversity in the religious background of members.

The earliest recorded group was founded in 1907; this was the Syrian Ladies Aid Society of New York, which raised funds to help needy immigrants from Greater Syria. In the next year the Syrian Merchants Association was formed, which initially only lasted for a few years, but was then reformed in 1929. The association represented dozens of smaller merchant associations around the city, and coordinated and represented their business interests. As many Arab immigrants to the United States first became involved in peddling and/or some sort of business (as grocers, dry goods salesmen, and importers), this association was an important forum for their local economic and political interests.

There was also the Beyrouth Young Men's Society, formed in Brooklyn in 1916, which was a charity and social activist club, primarily geared toward helping immigrants from the city of Beirut (in today's Lebanon). The Syrian Education Society was formed in 1916 in New York City and Boston simultaneously, and worked to assist Arab students in the United States, as well as promote lecture series. The Damascus Fraternity was formed in 1918 in Brooklyn, and it had a diverse (sectarian) membership that worked to help immigrants from the city of Damascus (in today's Syria). The American-Syrian Federation was also formed in Brooklyn in 1925, and it joined together smaller, but older sociopolitical organizations, some of which traced back to the first decade of the 20th century. They sought to protect and represent the rights and interests of Syrians in New York City. A similar organization was formed in 1928, called the Syrian Junior League.

Particular sectarian communities formed their own associations to promote their religious traditions and beliefs, as well as to give practical aid and support to members of their sect. One such group was the Syrian Catholic Association, Inc., which was formed in 1919 in Brooklyn and raised funds for charity and religious purposes. The Young Men's Muslim Association was also concerned with the moral and social well-being of young men and women. In 1928 two affiliated Maronite associations were created: Holy Trinity Young Men's Club and Holy Trinity Young Ladies League.

Historians generally feel that the more specific cultural and identity markers (accepting the label "Arab") as well as efforts to promote stronger bonds

Kahlil Gibran and Ameen Rihani

Perhaps the most famous Arab American active in the 1920s, and certainly the best known Mahjar poet in the Middle East, was Kahlil Gibran. Gibran was both an artist and writer, and he published various poetry and prose works in both English and Arabic in the first three decades of the 20th century. His best known work is *The Prophet* (1923), which was a huge success at the time, and remains an American classic. He has been described as a devotee of Romanticism and mysticism. No other Arab held such prominence in the United States for many decades. Gibran considered himself a man of two worlds, and he literally lived between many worlds, traveling back and forth between the United States, France, and his birthplace in Mount Lebanon.

Another prominent Arab-American writer of the period was Ameen Rihani, who was also born in Mount Lebanon. Perhaps in terms of his level of output in English and engagement with the major political and intellectual debates of the time, he should be considered even more important than Gibran. In 1903 he published his first book in English, a translation entitled *The Quatrains of Abul-'Ala*, in his attempt to cultivate an appreciation for Arabic literature in the United States. He continued publishing English- and Arabic-language works, and in 1911 he published *The Book of Khalid*, the first novel in English by an Arab American. His works are infused with a personal and philosophical spirit that characterized (some say influenced) the development of early Arab-American literature. In the 1920s he became motivated by a desire to bring the various political upheavals of the Middle East in the post–World War I period to the attention of the public in the United States, and he wrote a series of travelogues, political essays, and newspaper articles in English to these ends. Thus his writing from this time onward focused on the new postwar colonial order in the region being constructed by the British and French, the impact of Zionist settlement in Palestine, and studies on the new Arab leaders of the region. He, even more than Gibran, lived and traveled between the region and the United States.

Author Khalil Gibran posed in Middle Eastern clothing as a young man in 1898.

among the many different types of Arab Americans in the United States only began to emerge in the 1930s, and really accelerated after the creation of Israel in 1948. An important attempt to promote bonds among the variety of Arabs in the United States occurred in Boston in 1932, when a regional confederation of "Syrian" organizations was formed. This Eastern Federation sponsored social and cultural activities, created scholarships, and did outreach to non-Syrian communities. It served as a model for later regional "Syrian" federations. Yet a close look at the member organizations brings to the surface the overall state of the Arab-American communities: their leadership was U.S.-born and English-speaking, and cultural activities were primarily limited to Arabic food, music, and dance.

LITERATI AND CULTURAL ASSOCIATIONS

Due to their concentration in the East Coast of the United States, it is no surprise that New York City and Boston (as was the case for Kahlil Gibran), became the centers for Arab-American cultural and intellectual activities and societies. Furthermore, in Arab culture, poetry had long been deemed the highest art form, so poets, and other cultural elite, were held in high regard and performed important cultural and intellectual functions in a variety of venues. Writers, poets, and people who could recite the Qur'an in particular, were often seen as guardians of the Arabic language; oral recitations of poetry or the Qur'an were a normal part of any Arab social gathering. Finally, given the separation of Arab Americans from their people and culture back in the Arab world, these literati, newspapers, and cultural and intellectual associations were seen as maintaining an important bond with Arab civilization.

The earliest recorded such society was the Lebanon League of Progress, founded in 1911 in New York and active for many decades. It was closely affiliated with the *al-Huda* newspaper, thus a Maronite Christian organization, and promoted "Jihad for the sake of Lebanon." The word *jihad* has multiple meanings, but the implication here is that they worked to discuss and promote the nationalistic goals of Maronites in Mount Lebanon. Another similar organization, with a Syrian focus, was the Caravaneers, formed in 1919. A very interesting group was formed in Brooklyn in 1924 named the Book Club, which promoted literacy and education. They were especially interested in promoting the reading of books and discussions about the Middle East.

A man who made immense contributions to scholarly studies of the Middle East was Philip Hitti (1886–1978), whose teaching and/or publications groomed the next generations of historians and specialists on the Middle East. While he is better known for his historical studies, an important milestone was marked in 1924 when he published *The Syrians in America*, which has been called "the first systematic and scholarly study devoted to the Syrian immigration to the United States . . . [covering] not only historical, geographical, racial, social, religious, and economic background of the Syrians but also their status in America." Hitti

Rudolph Valentino and *The Sheik*

George Melford's silent movie *The Sheik* propelled little-known actor Rudolph Valentino (1895–1926) to stardom, creating the first Hollywood sex symbol. In his role in both *The Sheik* (1921) and *The Son of the Sheik* (1926), the handsome and suave Italy-born Valentino came to symbolize the "Dark Lover," exuding an erotic-exoticness that was both "Latin" and "Arab." The film grossed over $1 million due in part to the pre-existing fascination that the U.S. public had with "the Orient."

The movie was based on E. M. Hull's novel The Sheik (1919), which told the story of a tribal leader, Ahmed Ben Hassan, who kidnapped Lady Diana Mayo and absconded with her into the Sahara desert. Keeping her captive, he begins a physical relationship that initiates as rape but blossoms into a love affair. Ahmed is a dark, mysterious, virile antagonist who is out to conquer and dominate, but it is Diana who, in the end, tames his heart. This transformation is the overall theme of the book.

The book and movie, indeed women's obsession for Valentino, were products of the rapid social, gender, sexual, and racial debates of the period, often played out in the "safe" confines of literature and film. There are also themes of the West taming the East, or rather, civilizing the Easterner; Ahmed represents the dangerous and primitive East. On the other hand, the ending overturns these themes by revealing that Ahmed is actually an English noble, whom Diana marries, thus eliminating any possibility of miscegenation or illegitimate children (she was pregnant).

The movie spawned a craze for "Arab fashions." This craze added to the pre-existing 19th- and early 20th-century interest in the "Orient," which included imitations of clothing, furniture, dance, music and clothes from the lands of the Ottoman Empire (today's Middle East). The Roaring Twenties, already a time known for its exuberance and celebration of transgressions—whether this meant transgressing Prohibition or embracing African-American music—allowed for the expression of the unconventional and exotic through Orient-themed parties and clothing. Hull and Melford were continuing in the tradition of novels and films depicting "desert romances" and adventures in the Middle East, and they spawned even more, such as *The Sheikh's Wife* (1922), *The Arab* (1924), *The Thief of Baghdad* (1924), Valentino in *The Young Rajah* (1924) and his reprisal in *The Son of the Sheik* (1926), and *The Desert Song* (1929). This craze continued into the 1930s: there were over 40 films featuring Arabs 1930–34. However, even though many films with Arabs or Middle Eastern themes continued, and continue, to be made since the 1920 and 1930s, the image of Arabs has not changed: Arab characters represent threats of rape, violence, terrorism, theft, and sinister power. As multiple film historians have observed, stereotyping Middle Easterners is the one prejudice that is still allowed in Hollywood. In many ways, Valentino's aggressive sex-crazed Ahmed Ben Hassan is the most famous of these "reel Arabs."

taught at universities in Lebanon, and at Columbia University and Princeton University, and still remains a highly respected scholar.

The publication of Hitti's *The Syrians in America* indicates that the Arab-American community was becoming self-aware in the 1920s, and was more actively embracing its American identity. Arab-American writers in the 1930s and 1940s increasingly reflected this new reality in addition to the fact that more of their works were written in English. For example, Ashad Hawie (1888–1962) wrote of his experiences as a U.S. soldier in World War I in his 1942 autobiography *The Rainbow Ends.* He brought the contribution of his fellow Arab Americans in the war to the attention of the American public. In similar fashion, Salom Rizk wrote *Syrian Yankee* in 1943, which reproduces the classic "American story": from humble beginnings in Syria, he comes to the United States and becomes a citizen, faces the Depression, and all these experiences mold him into a typical American.

CULTURAL PRODUCTION

The first book printed in Arabic in the United States was a poetry collection by Mikha'il Rustum in 1895, entitled *al-Gharib fi al-gharb* ("The Stranger in the West"). This book was followed by works by Yusuf Nu'man al-Ma'luf and Salim Sarkis, and then both Ameen Rihani and Kahlil Gibran began publishing in 1902. Ameen Rihani holds the distinction of being the first Arab American to publish a work in English, which was *The Quatrains of Abul-'Ala* in 1903.

Despite the efforts of Arab literati, such as the members of al-Rabitah al-Qalamiyah, since the Arab community did not have many educational institutions in the United States that could maintain their linguistic and literary heritage, there was a slow atrophy of readers of Arabic (spoken Arabic, especially colloquial dialects, was much easier to retain). Difficulties of funding and acquiring the necessary technology (it was more difficult to get the specialized Arabic script printing presses that were necessary) and aspects of the diglossia in Arabic—which means there is a difference between the spoken forms of Arabic and the written, literary or journalistic form—also contributed to the decline. The first acknowledgement of this linguistic shift came in 1926 when the editors of *al-Huda* founded the English-language journal *Syrian World*, which was an effort to maintain communal bonds, even if done in English. *Syrian World* only lasted six years, but was a model for the later so-called ethnic press.

Up until the Great Depression, there was a steadily increasing amount of record labels in the United States that signed recording contracts with Arab musicians. In the 1930s, as record companies became less able to maintain many recording contracts, Arab Americans began to open their own recording labels. This period saw the success of labels such as Malouf, Macsoud, Maarouf, Ash Shark, and Alamphone. The 1930s also saw Arabic films produced in the Middle East (Egypt) shown in the United States for the first time, starting in 1934 at the Brooklyn Academy of Music.

CONCLUSION

One theme of the Arab-American experience in the first 40 years of the 20th century was the attempts to create more cross-sectarian and intra-cultural unity. However, local and familial loyalties still predominated, and it was only at the end of the 1930s and into the 1940s, with the growing politicization of the Arab-American community concurrent with its awareness of the plight of Palestinians and the rise of Arab nationalist ideologies in the Middle East, that these parochial cleavages in the Arab-American communities were more successfully bridged.

PETER C. VALENTI
NEW YORK UNIVERSITY

Further Reading

Abraham, Sameer Y. and N. Abraham. *Arabs in the New World: Studies on Arab-American Communities*. Detroit, MI: Wayne State University, 1983.

Benson, Kathleen and Philip M. Kayal, eds. *A Community of Many Worlds: Arab American in New York City*. New York: Museum of the City of New York, 2002.

Boosahda, Elizabeth. *Arab-American Faces and Voices: The Origins of an Immigrant Community*. Austin, TX: University of Texas Press, 2003.

Gualtieri, Sarah. "Becoming 'White': Race, Religion and the Foundations of Syrian/Lebanese Ethnicity in the United States." *Journal of American Ethnic History*, Vol. 20, No. 4, summer 2001.

Haddad, Y.Y., "Muslims in the United States," in *Islam: The Religious and Political Life of a World Community,* M. Kelly, ed. New York: Praeger, 1984.

Hitti, Philip K. *The Syrians in America*. New York: George H. Doran Co., 1924.

Hooglund, Eric. *Crossing the Waters: Arabic-Speaking Immigrants to the United States before 1940*. Washington, D.C.: Smithsonian Institution, 1987.

Hourani, Albert Habib and Nadim Shehadi, eds. *The Lebanese in the World: A Century of Emigration*. London: Centre for Lebanese Studies, 1992.

Ludescher, Tanyss. "From Nostalgia to Critique: An Overview of Arab American Literature." *Multi-Ethnic Literature of the United States (MELUS)*, Vol. 31, No. 4, winter 2006.

McCarus, Ernest. *The Development of Arab-American Identity*. Ann Arbor, MI: University of Michigan Press, 1994.

Moses, John G. *Annotated Index to the Syrian World, 1926–1932*. Saint Paul, MN: University of Minnesota, 1994.

Naff, Alixa. *Becoming American: The Early Arab Immigrant Experience*. Carbondale, IL: Southern Illinois University Press, 1993.

Popp, Richard Alan. "al-Rabitah al-Qalamiyah, 1916." *Journal of Arabic Literature*, Vol. 32, No. 1, 2001.

CHAPTER 4

World War II and the Forties: 1939 to 1949

THE SECOND WAVE of Arab immigration to the United States began after World War II, which brought momentous social and political developments, both in Arabic homelands and in the United States. These changes hewed a wide chasm between the immigrants from the first and second waves of Arab immigration—even between those who came from the same geographic region. In contrast to earlier arrivals, postwar Arab immigrants were more educated, politicized, and skilled. As nationals of various, and often competing, Arab nations that finally achieved independence only after the war, they were much more aware of international events than their earlier brethren. These political events in their homelands underpinned Arab nationalism and profoundly affected both the character and map of the Middle East.

The Immigration Act of 1924 (the Johnson-Reed Act) had set a quota on immigrants from each country in the world, except countries in northern and western Europe and in Asia. Each Arab country received the minimum quota of 100 new immigrants per year. Only the wives and dependent children of U.S. citizens could come to the United States without being blocked by these quotas. In addition to the quotas, the Great Depression of the 1930s and World War II in the early 1940s discouraged people from immigrating to the United States. After World War II many Arab immigrants who were

U.S. citizens sponsored their families to immigrate to the United States. Other Arab immigrants, usually the relatives of earlier immigrants, came under quotas. Still others, like immigrants from Jordan, started a new migration to the United States. Some Arabs came to the United States to advance their education on student visas, but often stayed after marriage to an American citizen or through an employer who sponsored them.

ARAB-AMERICAN IDENTITY AND ASSIMILATION

The term "Arab" only began to be commonly used to describe Arabic-speaking immigrants to the United States after World War II. Also, unlike their earlier countrymen, most of the immigrants of this period were Muslim. However, whether Muslim or Christian, Saudi Arabian or Syrian, they wished to be called Arabs. Unlike the pioneers who came between the 1880s and 1920, these more recent arrivals came to a United States that had experienced two World Wars; had struggled through an international economic depression; and had become the world's leading industrial, scientific, technological, and military power. The American-raised and American-born descendants of the early Arab pioneers inherited the task of bridging the chasm and coming to terms with the differences in the newly adopted nation of the United States. They began to stress the idea of Arab unity. The Arab identity they awoke to, however, was vastly different than what had been passed on to them by their parents and grandparents.

Arab assimilation into the mainstream of American society was a many-faceted process, moving unevenly and unpredictably throughout America's pluralistic, open, and diverse society. The complexities of assimilation were governed by a number of variables inherent in the migration of any given people: the period of migration; the social, political, and economic conditions in America; Arab cultural values and customs; Arab motivation for migrating and their expectations; and the degree of Arab nationalistic sentiments. In the decades leading up to World War II, Americanization was frequently pressed on immigrants by an uneasy and, at times, racially prejudiced American public. The pressure to assimilate intensified for Arab Americans until the tempering effects of the 1930s Great Depression.

More than a few immigrant groups, Arabs among them, willingly acquiesced to the concept of Americanization and, from their own perspective, to the benefits of becoming an American citizen. The assimilation process could be said for the most part to have begun in the homeland. When the decision to migrate was made, the prospective Arab migrants were carried to the edge of a new culture, tradition, history, and political system. Perceptions about American society and its employment opportunities, and the memorization of a few American words, stimulated their imagination and alerted the prospective emigrants to change. The anticipation of change and adaptation were part of the emigrants' tools of survival. It prepared them to face problems that might become a wedge

In the late 1930s Palestinians began to immigrate to the United States in slightly larger numbers than in previous years. The immigrants came from peasant backgrounds like this farmer threshing crops with cattle near Ramla in the British Mandate region in July 1938.

Palestinian Peasant Immigration

Although the first wave of Arab immigrants came mainly from Syria and Lebanon, Palestinians had begun to appear on American immigration records around the turn of the century. Toward the end of the 1930s, corresponding with the Arab rebellion of 1936–39, their immigration increased slightly, with numbers averaging about 250 a year. The low volume of migration was due to the economically depressed conditions of Palestinian peasants, who were oppressed by absentee landlords, and perhaps also due to the lack of communication between the Palestine province and Syria, the largest source of Middle Eastern migration to America. The average Syrian peasant, in contrast, was a landowner; his relationship with the land was, on the whole, more pragmatic, physical, and economic than emotional, as land could easily be replaced. It is also likely that the lower numbers of Palestinian immigrants in the United States were also due to the fact that much of the Palestinian chain migration had been directed more to South America than to North America. Even so, by 1936, the number of Palestinian immigrants in the United States exceeded the number of Syrian and Lebanese immigrants for the first time.

between themselves and their families' basic needs and goals. In this process, a few Old World values were changed in the process of Americanization.

ADAPTATION

Following the patterns of adaptation to the new society, parents began to relax their control over their children. Daughters were allowed some freedom in their choice of husbands, education, music, and food, and the interethnic marriages of sons were accepted as mere minor calamities. But as long as there remained a nucleus of native values that resisted assimilation into American society, full assimilation was not to be achieved. For Arabs, the granite block of values—the essence of being Arab—was the nexus of behavioral patterns that protected and perpetuated family honor, values, tradition, and unity. This included the patriarchal nature of much of Arab society, with its negative aspects such as violence against women and "honor killings."

Because older siblings intimately shared that pioneer experience in the new country with their parents and adhered more tightly to traditional values, the cultural gap between older, American-born or foreign-born siblings and the youngest, American-born siblings—growing up at a later stage in their parents' American experience—could be as broad as that between younger siblings and their immigrant parents.

Inevitably, the extent of adjustment required to survive in the new country far exceeded any immigrant group's imagination and preparation; adjustment sometimes met with resistance, caused emotional pain, and resulted in indifference. Arab Americans learned the English language through education and employment, attended citizenship classes, and acquired American manners and material possessions for attracting a measure of acceptance in the new society. Whenever these accomplishments became accepted within the group, as symbols of status and barometers of success, they were pursued with even greater vigor. Before World War II, the American attitude toward the Americanization of foreigners required, to a large degree, social and cultural conformity of immigrants in the newly adopted land. By and large, the aliens were expected to be happy to shed their native identity for the privilege of participating in American blessings and success. The Arabs' acceptance of America as their permanent home was signaled by establishment of such institutions as Eastern-rite churches, an Arabic-language press, social clubs, and several educational and charitable associations, mainly in the more populous East Coast urban colonies.

Syrian immigrants of the late 19th and early 20th centuries were not economically, religiously, or politically displaced peasants. Although they derived from a lower economic scale of society, they came voluntarily and enthusiastically. It was the desire and drive to succeed that motivated Arab immigrants to take this journey, and reject the oppressive policies that other immigrants faced in their own homelands. For many Arab immigrants, quick-wealth opportunities to promote family status translated into zealous ambition. This

Arab groups continued to build bonds through community groups like this early 1940s Arab merchant's association after they immigrated.

reality was recognized by the Egyptian poet Hafiz Ibrahim, who wrote in a poem before World War I: "if they thought there was a livelihood to be made there, the Lebanese would surely migrate to Mars."

NEW OPPORTUNITIES

When Arab Americans sought explanations for what perplexed them, they turned to veteran immigrants and the Arabic press. These natural leaders tended to interpret American life from the stories they heard from earlier migrants, through the media, and through myths of an older America, rather than through the comprehension of the issues that loomed large for the native population. Furthermore, the second wave of Arab immigrants, inspired by the financial possibilities as well as their release from their homeland's social, political, and economic restrictions, carried with them an emerging conception of America that helped them overlook its flaws.

To establish a strong foothold in the United States, intermarriage between settlements reinforced ties between new and remote settlements and the more established communities. The proliferation of settlements not only opened up greater opportunities for new arrivals, but also constituted undeniable evidence of the Arabs' belief in the promise of America. Old ways of

Arab Americans in World War II

Fighter pilot James Jabara, who flew in combat in World War II and the Korean War, in the 1940s.

The Arabs' attitude toward President Franklin Roosevelt was nearly universally positive. Regardless of class, income, or occupation, they admired his compassion for the downtrodden and his extended hand to the immigrant. Although there are no accurate numbers for Arab Americans serving in the armed forces, several thousand Arab Americans served the United States in both World War I and World War II. However, a reasonable estimate counts at least 30,000 GIs of Arab lineage who fought for the United States against Hitler, Mussolini, and the emperor of Japan. In fact, America's first World War II flying ace was Col. James Jabara. A native of Wichita, Kansas, and of Lebanese background, Jabara would later shoot down 15 Russian MiG planes in the Korean War. He was awarded two Distinguished Flying Crosses, and in 1950 was named by the Air Force Association as its most distinguished aviator.

Another young Arab-American, Najeeb Halaby, a young officer from Dallas with a Syrian-Lebanese father, aided the war effort in unusual ways. When America entered World War II, Najeeb joined the Navy as an aviator, where he test-piloted the first U.S. jet plane. He helped organize the Navy's first test pilot school, and was a test pilot for the first operational U.S. jet plane, the *Bell P-59*. Halaby's glorious and historic moment as an aviator, however, came just before the end of the war in the Lockheed *Shooting Star*. On May 1, 1945, Halaby took off from Muroc AFB, California, and arrived five hours and 40 minutes later in Patuxent, Maryland—the first transcontinental jet flight in U.S. history.

Other activities in which Arab Americans contributed to the war effort included Syrian Red Cross fundraising drives and War Bonds drives run by the Syrian-Palestinian Committee, one of which aimed for a $2 million goal. This community in Brooklyn had already raised millions for the war effort, and was officially thanked by the Treasury Department. George Hamid, the circus impresario and owner of Atlantic City's Million-Dollar Pier and Steel Pier, raised $300,000 from the theater industry as chairman of the Army-Navy Emergency Relief Society. He was also appointed by the Navy Relief Society as general chairman of outdoor amusements.

seeing themselves, notably as transients with limited goals, were supplanted by the dynamics of new opportunities. The central concern continued to be upward mobility. With a more certain American focus, a Syrian middle class was slowly and steadily taking shape. Prosperity and advancement became more common. Building on their prewar progress, they became owners of small businesses, acquired homes in better neighborhoods, and concerned themselves with their children's futures.

Postwar communities resembled Syrian villages less; the pioneer's feelings of foreignness were gradually being replaced by a sense of being American; and Syrians began addressing the increasing complexities of American society and accommodating themselves on an unprecedented scale. Consequently, Syrian society appeared to be finding equilibrium between the predominant American values and steadily eroding native values. Yet the distinction between the prewar and postwar Syrian society was in some respects a broad chasm, and for others a narrow path. Not ones to gamble, the Syrians, holding firmly to their habits of hard work and parsimony, reoriented their goals toward a successful future in America.

PUSH AND PULL FACTORS DURING THE SECOND WAVE

The second wave of Arab immigration, which began after World War II, was 60 percent Muslim. The time between 1938 and 1948 is best characterized as a period of growth, mainly among Lebanese immigrants. The period from 1948 to 1960 was a primary growth period for all Arab nationality groups, with a marked increase in Muslim immigrants. Many other Arabs came to large American cities such as New York, Boston, Cleveland, Chicago, Detroit, and Los Angeles as refugees, like the Palestinians who were dispossessed of their land following 1948 and the first Arab-Israeli war. With few exceptions, it is difficult to estimate the size of any particular group of early immigrants. The size of each nationality group and the community as a whole had to be large enough, however, to support the religious institutions that were established during the early years.

The first Lebanese Maronite church, for example, was erected on Detroit's East Congress Street in 1916. Likewise, what became known as the Mother Mosque of America in Cedar Rapids, Iowa, was built in 1934, and was the first permanent structure to be built specifically to serve as a mosque in the United States. Both of these institutions testify to the existence of a sizeable Arab population following the first wave of Arab immigration. Like earlier groups, pre–World War II Arabs migrated to the United States for a combination of pushing and pulling factors.

In 1947 the newly formed United Nations divided Palestine into a Jewish state and an Arab state. Then in 1948, Zionists in Palestine declared the independent Jewish state of Israel. War immediately broke out, which the Israelis won, adding more territory under their control. Although some 800,000

Palestinians became refugees, there was a strong Palestinian determination to stay on their land to keep it from being confiscated by the Israeli government. Eventually, some of these refugees immigrated to several countries, including the United States.

For the earliest Arab immigrants, the Syrian-Lebanese immigrated mainly for economic reasons: the destruction of the once-prosperous silk industry, limited landholding on inhospitable mountain soil, heavy taxation, and occasional drought worked to push the peasantry from the land. On the other side of the world, however, there was an expanding American economy, which was the principal pull force for most early Arab immigrants. Economic considerations continued to predominate Arabs' decision to immigrate in the post–World War II period. As soon as some arrivals established themselves in the United States, they sent away for family members and relatives back home, and began a process of family chain migration that is still very much in evidence today. With time it became clear to many immigrants that their family's temporary status in America was becoming transformed into a permanent one, either by design or by forces outside their control. Assisting family members in immigrating also allowed families to reestablish themselves in the United States. Other immigrants aided family members, kinsmen, and fellow countrymen to migrate in order to assist them in family stores and other economic ventures.

ADJUSTMENTS AND SOLIDARITY

These new Arab immigrants were not free from suffering during their adjustment process in the new country. The realization of the problems of Arab-American youth brought about certain adjustments, requiring scattered Arab families through marriage ties and other social needs from across the nation to unify, creating a new racial solidarity.

One adjustment was related to religious practices. Under pressure to abandon or alter their faiths to conform to American mores, Arab immigrants adjusted their religious practices as they adapted to a new environment. Similarly, Arab Americans succeeded in diversifying the religious landscape of America during this period. Among the pre–World War II immigrants from the Arab world, the majority were Christians, mainly from the area of Mount Lebanon. While some of these early immigrants were mobile peddlers and tradespeople, others settled in cities, towns, and rural areas in Middle America.

Arab-American Christians established their own churches as a central part of their new communities. Arab-American Christians and Muslims went to a church or mosque for religious worship, as well as to make friends or meet a potential spouse from a similar community, cultural, and historical background. Churches and mosques were also used for instruction in the Arabic language and to host various kinds of celebrations, including weddings.

Second Wave Push vs. First Wave Pull

The second wave of Arab immigration to America, spurred in part by the occupation of Palestine, also included the beginning of what would later be called the "brain drain" from newly independent Arab states, such as Egypt, Syria, Iraq, Jordan, and the North African Arab countries. A "brain drain" is characterized as the regional departure of persons with education, technical skills, and knowledge. Some were dissatisfied with the series of coups that occurred frequently in these newly created states, some wanted a better standard of living, and some were political exiles from intra-Arab squabbles and the Arab-Israeli crisis. Much distinguishes the Palestinian and other Arab immigrants in the second wave from their forefathers in the first wave. The search for a better livelihood was the primary pull for most early Syrians to come to the United States, with political deterioration and warfare a secondary push.

These factors were reversed for second wave Arabs, who, arriving in the United States after 1948, were compelled to emigrate because of crises at home. Unlike the first wave, many were refugees and exiles who had lost a land that would be transformed beyond recognition. The second wave immigrants arrived more often by plane than by boat, and tended to be in a much better financial position than the early turn-of-the-century Arabs. These second wave immigrants were also better educated than the earlier group, whose members were overwhelmingly illiterate before coming to the United States. This combination of distinctive differences between the second wave and the first wave kept the two communities separate for many years, until the 1970s. The second wave Arab Americans had more reasons to be grateful to the United States than the previous group, since as exiles from war and political upheaval, many found the United States a secure haven to work, live, and maintain their religions and cultural heritage. Their superior education and skills helped them adapt to a sophisticated postwar American society more quickly than their peddler and factory laborer forebears.

However, this was not always the case. First, the skills they carried to the New World, which initially eased them into U.S. society, also led them into social structures, such as conservative workplaces, that required them to hide their views. Second, because 60 percent of the second wave immigrants were Muslim, many were more spiritually alienated from mainstream America than the first wave immigrants. Third, Palestinians, drawn by U.S. freedom, were concomitantly repelled by U.S. policies, and this made for more mixed feelings than in the early-wave immigrants and their progeny. Fourth, whereas early Arab immigrants and their offspring shared in the wholesale adaptation to the mores of America, second wave immigrants kept "their bags packed" much longer because their journey was supposed to have been temporary. Fifth, the alienation the second wave immigrants carried with them into U.S. society was not alleviated by interaction with the earlier Syrian-Lebanese immigrants, as they did not often socialize with each other.

However, early Muslim immigrants faced grave problems establishing Islam. Mostly uneducated and unacquainted with American culture, they felt discrimination in their jobs and in their efforts to erect houses for prayer. Zoning laws sometimes obstructed them from constructing mosques in the United States. They found themselves unable to teach Islam to their children for want of materials in English. Muslims were also hampered in fulfilling their prayer obligations, which required praying five times a day at prescribed times, including noon and early afternoon, because they often faced ridicule or pressure from their peers. Although the number of mosques and Islamic centers continued to increase, the dispersal speeded the process of acculturation and led to local innovations.

Where chain migration had occurred in cities like Cedar Rapids, Iowa; Detroit, Michigan; and Toledo, Ohio, Arab-American Muslims were able to organize institutions early. Family ties, shared experiences, and common outlook helped weld the community together. The second and third generations, while committed to their Arab-Islamic identity, were anxious to maintain their American roots. Thus, differences between American-born Muslims and those who were raised overseas continued to be a source of strain, each group fervently believing that their worldview was ultimately better for the future of the community. Muslims experienced a considerable amount of prejudice in the United States. In addition to general public ignorance about the teachings of Islam, there was an accumulated heritage of mistrust that had lingered since the Crusades of the European Middle Ages.

THE SEARCH FOR A BETTER LIFE

Immigrants to the United States arrived from a number of countries, bringing with them different languages, cultures, and traditions. Despite these differences, they had one thing in common: the search for a better life. Immigrants hoped to achieve, through work, a level of economic prosperity unknown in their own land. Because many were able to accomplish this, the United States earned the name "the land of opportunity." While the majority of the first wave of Arab immigrants were employed, many quickly began to invest in their own businesses, primarily revolving around selling goods, and became known for their ability to operate them successfully. Some sold household items door-to-door, while others opened grocery and produce stores. Because of this, Arab Americans became known for their entrepreneurial spirit, exemplified by New York Arab-American merchants. During this time many changes occurred in the Arab American community. As the community evolved, its work patterns changed as well. The children of earlier immigrants were able to pursue professional careers different from their parents, thanks to higher education and the familiarity of American language and culture. But new arrivals continued to come from the Arab world and fill the vacancies left by older immigrants, keeping many of the entrepreneurial traditions alive.

Arab Americans became leaders in the United Auto Workers' union after its founding in 1935, and continued to work in manufacturing in the 1930s and 1940s. These men were machining the firing end of a U.S. Army 40 mm. anti-aircraft gun barrel in a Chrysler plant that had been converted for wartime production in Highland Park, Detroit, around 1942.

Following World War II, the predominantly Muslim Arab immigrants from Lebanon, Palestine, Egypt, Syria, Iraq, and Yemen often held professional degrees in medicine, law, and engineering, and came from an urban middle- and upper-middle-class background. These immigrants maintained strong ties to their national and Arab identities, but not necessarily to their religion. In other words, they were often secular in their world views. Although most adapted to the American way of life, they continued to identify with the Arab world and to speak Arabic in the home. Because of their educational and professional background, many of these Arab immigrants were able to live in more affluent suburban areas and to choose good school districts for their children.

The generation of Syrian Americans who were the first to be born on American soil, and who came of age during the Depression and World War II, were perhaps the most Americanized and assimilated of all Arab-American groups. They embraced many social clubs such as the Kiwanis, Rotary Clubs, Masonic orders, and PTAs. They were full-fledged members of their church boards and helped enhance the reputation of their mosques. First-genera-tion Syrian and Lebanese Americans were the ones who first introduced the terms "Syrian" and "Lebanese" into the American vocabulary, elevating the American consciousness of the Arab world beyond deserts, strife, and belly dancers. Because their efforts at Americanization were at the highest levels of society and their chosen fields, the images they projected helped deter-mine Americans' perception of Arab values and beliefs.

COHESION THROUGH SOCIAL LIFE, ART, MEDIA, AND CULTURE

To maintain Arab identity and group cohesion, beginning in the 1930s, local social clubs and churches serving immigrants recognized the benefit of com-ing together to share cultural expression. As America was becoming more tol-erant and welcoming of non-European cultures and communities, a crisis was created. By the 1930s Arab-American community groups began to organize music parties and festivals for which they hired professional musicians. Live music performances became the focus of two events in the Arab-American community: the *hafla*, a cross between a concert and a party; and the *mahra-jan*, an outdoor festival that could last for three days and involved hundreds, and sometimes thousands, of participants.

The idea behind the hafla was to celebrate a community event, raise funds for charity, or just to have people come together for a good time. Later, as communities grew and the hafla became more popular, they were held in ho-tel ballrooms that could accommodate larger groups of 1,000 to 1,500 people. Gradually, the hafla evolved into a formal musical event during which the community gathered to listen to live performances of Syrian, Egyptian, and Lebanese music and enjoy skits, poetry, and speeches from clergymen and community leaders. The hafla became an important institution in the life of the community. The mahrajan, or community festival, started as a church picnic where musicians would play, people would dance, and the older folks would tell stories to the young. The mahrajan was also a social affair where making friends, matchmaking, eating, and dancing were as important as the live music.

In the years following World War II, the many Muslim and pan-Arab na-tionalists who immigrated to the United States believed in Arab unity and solidarity. These newcomers felt that the mainstream American press did not represent their concerns, and they looked toward the Arabic press as a source of unbiased news about the Arab world, particularly the Arab-Israeli conflict and their situation in their new country. American-born Arabs who felt con-nected to their ancestral homelands needed a press that could communicate to them in English. As a result, the publishers and editors of the new press worked to develop Arab-American community solidarity by providing infor-mation in both English and Arabic, and paved the way for other forms of me-dia later in the century.

CONCLUSION

The 1940s era of Arab-American history was mainly one of assimilation and acculturation. The lack of newcomers from back home created a vacuum of communication between the Arab world and the community in the United States. Most Arab Americans modified their cultural traditions and outlooks somewhat and made changes in their lives accordingly. Many assimilated into the mainstream, becoming invisible as an ethnic minority and deemphasizing their ethnic backgrounds at home, as well as in public. After World War II, revolutions and wars dominated the political and economic realities in Arab world. Some Arab elites immigrated to America as political exiles, especially from Iraq, Egypt, and Palestine. These exiled elites arrived educated with strong English-language skills and vast resources, and generally moved to cosmopolitan areas.

KHODR M. ZAAROUR
SHAW UNIVERSITY AND NORTH CAROLINA CENTRAL UNIVERSITY

Further Reading

Arab American Institute. "The Najeeb Halaby Award for Public Service." Available online, URL: www.aaiusa.org/foundation/1035/najeeb-halaby-award. Accessed March 25, 2009.

Boosahad, Elizabeth. *Arab-American Faces and Voices: The Origins of an Immigrant Community.* Austin, TX: University of Texas Press, 2003.

Hooglund, Eric J. *Crossing the Waters.* Washington, D.C.: Smithsonian Institution Press, 1987.

Kayyali, Randa A. *The Arab Americans: The New Americans.* Westport, CT: Greenwood Press, 2006.

Los Angeles Times. "Najeeb Halaby, 87; FAA Chief, Father of Queen Noor of Jordan." Available online, URL: http://articles.latimes.com/2003/jul/04/local/me-halaby4. Accessed March 25, 2009.

Naff, Alixa. *Becoming American: The Early Arab Immigrant Experience.* Carbondale, IL: Southern Illinois University Press, 1985.

Orfalea, Gregory. *Before the Flames: A Quest for the History of Arab Americans.* Austin, TX: University of Texas Press, 1988.

———. *The Arab Americans.* Northampton, MA: Interlink Publishing, 2006.

Schur, Joan Broadsky. *The Arabs: Coming to America.* Detroit, MI: Thomson/Gale, 2005.

Younis, Adele L. *The Coming of the Arabic-Speaking People to the United States.* New York: Library of Congress, 1995.

CHAPTER 5

The Fifties: 1950 to 1959

THE SECOND WAVE of Arab immigration to the United States lasted from 1947 to 1968, consisted of about 80,000 immigrants, and considerably changed the makeup of Arab America. While the first wave immigrants were primarily Christian and Syrian, and in search of better economic opportunities, economic considerations were secondary to the Muslim immigrants who made up 60 percent of the second wave. Most were Palestinians, Egyptians, Iraqis, Lebanese, and Yemeni. Many were from religious minorities in their own countries, and were looking for a more amenable home. More likely to be fleeing political upheaval and war, many of the second wave immigrants were in better financial shape than the average immigrant of any origin. They were also better educated and overwhelmingly literate, owing to the changes that had been wrought in the world over the 20th century.

WORLD EVENTS
A number of key events around the world, and particularly in the Middle East, had a profound influence on the pattern of Arab immigration to the United States. The post–World War II end of the colonialism era in the Arab world, and the shift toward the independence of various Arab states (whose borders were nevertheless those that had been determined by European powers) led many Arabs and onlookers to believe that a unified Arab state was close on

the horizon. Those who supported or actively worked toward this end were called pan-Arab nationalists, meaning that the "nationalism" to which they subscribed referred to the collective nation of the Arab peoples, not any particular existing Arab state. The political systems established in these early days reflected anti-imperialist sentiments, renewed Arab nationalism, and in some cases adopted aspects of socialism. Rarely were democratic institutions put in place.

Though foreign powers relinquished their control over the area, no one had any illusions that the Arab world would be left to its own devices. The area was blessed with natural resources (most obviously oil), the Suez Canal was critical to trade, and the Cold War was heating up in the 1950s, with the Middle East as a potential battleground for proxy wars.

ISRAEL

Palestine is a special case in the history of the post–World War II Arab world. Formerly under British control, it was converted into the new state of Israel, reviving the ancient homeland of the Jews. Though officially Britain did nothing but relinquish control over Palestine, as other European powers were relinquishing control over their various territories, the newly formed United Nations (UN) was strongly influenced by the British and the Americans, and the creation of Israel has generally been perceived as an Anglo-American action. The UN partitioned Palestine into seven parts, administering the Jerusalem/Bethlehem area itself, and dividing the remaining six equally among the Palestinian Arabs and the Jews. The Palestinian Arabs rejected the partitioning, while the Palestinian Jews embraced the plan and declared the independence of Israel as of 1948.

An Arab coalition of armies from Syria, Lebanon, Jordan, Egypt, and Iraq declared war on Israel in the name of reclaiming Palestinian lands, a plan that backfired—most of the combat occurred in Palestinian-controlled areas, wreaking havoc there, and Israel successfully defended itself and expanded its territory beyond the UN partition. Jordan annexed the West Bank, Egypt established rule over the Gaza Strip, and the state of Palestine ceased to exist as a political entity. Meanwhile, Jews around the world—mostly those living in Arab nations at first—moved to Israel, and an armistice was signed among all parties except Iraq in 1949. Most of the native Palestinian population, though, was displaced, seeking temporary lodging in neighboring Arab states or in the Egyptian- and Jordanian-controlled areas.

THE SECOND WAVE

The second wave immigrants were more equipped to integrate into American society, more likely to speak English, more likely to be professionals or skilled laborers, and therefore more likely to become a part of the American middle class that was so prominent in the 1950s. At the same time, the differences between the second wave immigrants and their American neighbors—including their first wave neighbors—could be profound. The U.S. population knew little about Islam, but the 1950s were an especially conservative time, with fundamentalism on the rise. This was a time when Jews were still excluded from many social clubs, and when many Christian Americans defended such policies (or the right of businesses to have such policies) regardless of political persuasion. Christian fundamentalism and evangelical churches were significantly on the rise, in contrast to the more liberal religious values that had prevailed in the century preceding World War II. It was a time when U.S. Senator Joseph McCarthy successfully held the spotlight on the national stage while accusing various individuals and classes of being communist infiltrators, on little to no evidence—a time when to be different could mean drawing suspicion.

In many cases, second wave immigrants may not have considered the United States a permanent home, and may not have tried as hard to acclimate and integrate. They were referred to as the ones who "still had their bags packed," and returned home frequently if possible, or to visit family in other countries. If political turmoil was their reason for relocation, they often expected to return home when things had settled down, particularly if the side favorable to them proved the eventual victor. Apart from attending the same places of worship, first and second wave Arab immigrants did

Festivals and Foods of Home

Outdoor festivals that were at their height of popularity in the decades before the Arab-American community began to call itself the Arab-American community—before the onset of pan-Arab-American identity—mahrajans were an early form of this awareness of shared heritage. While churches and mosques specific to religious groups, and social clubs and ladies' aid societies specific to nationality groups, were the main loci of Arab-American socializing outside the household, mahrajans appealed across religious and country-of-origin lines. Muslims and Christians, Lebanese and Egyptians, all attended the same festivals, which were commonly held in city parks and other locations, the same spaces used by traveling carnivals and the like.

Mahrajans were often three-day festivals, generally Friday through Sunday, featuring music, singing, and dancing all day and through much of the evening. Those attending could learn to play traditional Arab musical instruments, and to perform traditional dances. Traditional foods were served, a particular attraction for single men who had immigrated to the United States alone and were otherwise doing without the foods of home.

not intermingle much in the 1950s. The term "Arab American" did not even come into vogue until later years; during the second wave, there was rarely any collective reference to encompass Syrian Americans, Palestinian Americans, Lebanese Americans, Iraqi Americans, Egyptian Americans, and so on. They were people of different nationalities, traditions, and religions, though they recognized that they had things in common, just like European Americans did.

Many of the second wave immigrants continued to uphold old country values and practices, and expected their children to do the same. This especially affected women, since one of the key social differences between the United States and the Middle East was the modesty of women. Arab parents often expected their daughters to dress and behave modestly: no shorts, pants, or sleeveless dresses; no speaking to men on the street whether strangers or friends; and no raising their voices in public.

Many of those associated with deposed or threatened regimes in the Middle East immigrated to the United States, constituting an elite and often moneyed class of Arab immigrant. Quite often these Arabs established new communities, or moved into non-Arab communities (not necessarily assimilating in the process), rather than moving into the neighborhoods already settled by Arab Americans—too often those existing neighborhoods were poorer than the standard of living the new immigrants were accustomed to, though they might well find themselves in the same mosques as their less well-off countrymen.

IMMIGRANTS AND AMERICAN POLICIES

Furthermore, many second wave immigrants disagreed strongly with American policies. Palestinian Americans are the best example of this: the very conditions that had brought them to the United States were caused or supported by the United States, the most influentially pro-Israel country in the world. In a further irony, the creation of Israel had been promoted so strongly by the United States in part because one of the alternatives was so unappealing to Washington: opening the doors of immigration to the displaced Jews of the world, who could have settled in the West without displacing existing populations to the extent that they did in the Middle East.

About a quarter of second-wave immigration was Palestinian, though some of them came to the United States from countries of first refuge (other Arab countries like Lebanon, where they had initially hoped to find homes and work, before deciding to move on). Though immigration legislation passed in the 1920s set quotas on the number of immigrants that could be admitted from various countries (deliberately reflecting a western European bias), with the 1953 Refugee Relief Act, refugees were no longer counted toward those quotas. Thousands of Palestinians immigrated to the United States following the passage of the act, just as they were fleeing the former

Palestine for so many other parts of the globe. They called the 1948 war *al-Nakba*—"the Catastrophe."

RELIGIOUS MINORITIES: THE DRUZE

More than half of the Arab immigrants in the second wave were mainstream Muslims. However, greater percentages of smaller groups (that is, greater shares of those groups' total populations) immigrated, representing important shifts in the population distributions of those groups, as they became uncomfortable in or ostracized from their original homes in the Arab world, often as a result of political turmoil.

The Druze people are part of an Islamic denomination that is sometimes considered a separate religion because of the other elements the group has adopted. Many of the Arab Muslims who immigrated to the United States in the first wave were Druze, as the denomination has the most followers in Syria. Lebanese and Jordanian Druze began immigrating in greater numbers as part of the second and third waves.

Beginning as a Shi'a sect in the early 11th century, the Druze take an esoteric approach to Islamic foundations that is similar to that of the mystical sects of other faiths. The fashionable interest in gnosticism in the field of history has occasionally led to grouping the Druze in with the Gnostics, which is misleading; many sects and religious groups have emphasized the importance of intuition to religious understanding, and have taught that their sacred texts contained esoteric levels of meaning accessible only to the especially wise or insightful. In their retreat from the polytheism that pervaded in much of the pre- and non-Muslim world, the Druze strip God of all nameable attributes; there is no aspect of God, no way to describe God, except to simply say that he is God. To call him merciful, just, or mysterious would only humanize and anthropomorphize him. Though God thus transcends all attributes,

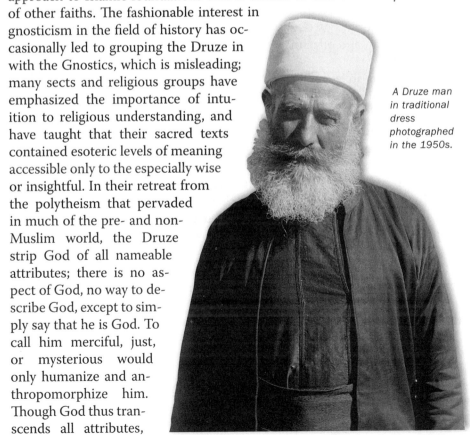

A Druze man in traditional dress photographed in the 1950s.

the light of God can be experienced by mystics, without God being limited by their experience of him—just as a mirror can contain your image but does not constrict you in doing so.

Most Druze are called *al-Juhhal*, "the ignorant"—the laity, the average Joe. The remaining fifth or so are the *al-Uqqal*, "the wise," who include both men and women, and who wear special clothes in keeping with the traditions of the Qur'an. The divide between the ignorant and the wise is not quite like that between laity and priests in other religions, nor the average Muslims and the religious leaders of the rest of Islam. While the Druze faith calls for celibacy and abstinence from tobacco, coffee, and alcohol, whether or not one must abide by all restrictions and requirements depends on whether one is ignorant or wise. The ignorant may ignore all religious behavioral requirements except for personal prayer, without being considered impious; the wise, on the other hand, must strictly adhere to the code. The levels of esoteric meaning of Druze belief and scriptures are known only to the wise; the ignorant do not even have access to the scriptures. This has led to a number of misunderstandings about Druze belief among non-Druze—for instance, many Arabs believe the Druze believe in reincarnation, which is simply an interpretation made by several Druze teachers over the years, not part of official teachings. A source of friction, though, is the lack of fasting during Ramadan and pilgrimages to Mecca—eliminating two of the five pillars of Islam.

Like Muslims in general, the Druze believe that—although the present form of their religion dates to the 11th century—theirs is a people and a tradition that extends back thousands of years to the early days of man. Conversion to the Druze faith is not permitted; one can only be born into it. For this reason, marriage to members of other faiths is discouraged, though it is not forbidden; the children of such a marriage are allowed to be raised as Druze. Not all Druze self-identify as Muslims; the tradition of Taqiya, adapted from the Shi'a, calls for concealing beliefs when necessary to avoid persecution, but even outside of that tradition, some Druze consider their faith a separate religion that developed out of Islam.

RELIGIOUS MINORITIES: THE ALAWI

Coming mostly from the northern highlands of Syria and Lebanon, the Alawi are a denominational offshoot from Shi'a Islam, elevating the first Shi'a Imam, Ali ibn Abi Talib, to a quasi-divine position. Like the Druze, they do not make their sacred texts available except to a special class of initiates, and they do not accept converts. They are often accused of deviating too severely from the basic tenets of Islam to be considered Muslims, an accusation that was especially common in the 1950s, but despite their lack of mosques (which made immigration an easier proposition for them), they do espouse the five pillars of Islam. A significant difference from mainstream Islam is the Alawi contention that the pillars should not—and cannot—be performed by everyone. Alawi contend that to view the pillars that way smacks of ritual power, of a secret formula that will enable the performer to enter Heaven; instead, the Alawi believe every individual's life and behavior should be guided by the example of Ali ibn Abi Talib and the prophet Muhammad.

Though Alawi eventually came to power in Syria (still a small minority, but politically influential), a disproportionate number of the Syrian immigrants in the 1950s were Alawi leaving the country in the midst of the political turmoil caused by the military coups of 1949 and the rise of the socialist Ba'ath party.

RELIGIOUS MINORITIES: THE COPTS

Copts are Egyptian Christians, the largest Christian group in the Arab World. Nearly all of them—around 90 percent—are members of the Coptic Orthodox Church, while the rest are Catholic or Protestant. Interestingly, the word *Copt* is derived from the Latinization of the Arabic word for "Egyptian."

The Copts are one of the oldest Christian communities in the world, Christianity having been introduced in the city of Alexandria during the first generation after the death of Jesus and spreading throughout Egypt fast enough that the Christian writings found by archaeologists in Oxyrhynchus are among the oldest in history. Originally an urban religion, Christianity spread to Egypt's rural areas in the second century, and Christian scriptures were translated into the Coptic language. Founding fathers of Christianity like Origen and Clement taught at the school in Alexandria. By the next century, Christians constituted the majority of the Egyptian population—though in Egypt's long history since, Christians have become a minority of about a fifth of the population, their numbers first dwindling with the Arab invasion in 641.

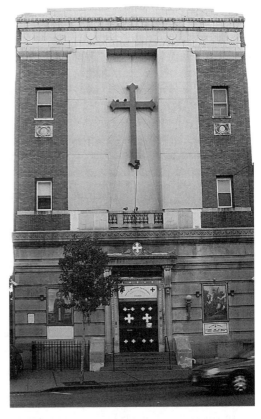

A Coptic Orthodox church in Jersey City, New Jersey, where Coptic Christians from Egypt now worship.

In 1952 Gamal Abdel Nasser led the Egyptian Revolution to seize control of the government, abolishing the monarchy and establishing a republic, first under the rule of General Muhammad Naguib and then under Nasser himself. Copts were marginalized by the new government, their rights restricted, and those who could afford to left in large numbers.

RELIGIOUS MINORITIES: THE CHALDEANS AND NESTORIANS

A significant number of the Arab Christians who immigrated to the United States were Chaldeans, many of them settling in and around Chicago and Detroit. The Chaldean Catholic Church is an Eastern church maintaining full communion with the Roman Catholic Church, meaning that both the Eastern and Western churches consider themselves equal and compatible, unified as a single religious entity. The Chaldean Catholic Church is therefore a "particular church," which in Catholicism means a church (not a single place of worship, but a denominational network thereof) that embodies the Catholic Church in a specific region, or for a specific culture. There tend to be minor differences in the liturgy and in the wording used for rites—and the Chaldean Catholic Church uses Syriac or Aramaic instead of Latin—but the essential tenets of belief are the same as in all Catholic churches.

There is a history of christological differences—theological disputes over the nature of Christ—between the Eastern and Western churches. In the 1950s more often than today, "Chaldean" frequently referred to the Nestorians of the Arab world, who teach that Christ existed as two persons, the divine perpetual Logos (the Son of God, who is the same as the Word discussed in the Gospel of John) and the mortal human Jesus; the Logos inhabited Jesus until his death. The belief is identified with Nestorius, the Archbishop of Constantinople in the early 5th century, but did not originate with him. At that early point in Christianity's history, there were many varied beliefs about Christ and God: some factions believed the God who was the Father of Jesus was not the same as the God of the Jewish Scriptures who led the Jews to Israel (of those, some argued there were two Gods; others argued that the Jewish God did not exist), some believed Jesus was mortal and susceptible to sin, and many believed that Jesus was not the biological son of God, but had rather been adopted by God as an adult. The minority position that Mary remained a virgin for life and had been conceived immaculately was adopted as official church doctrine.

Nestorius, then, did not stand out at the time. But the formation of the early Churches in both the East and the West—joining together the many local religious communities in unity—meant picking interpretations of scripture and sticking to them, and attempting to convince those who did not agree. Those attempts were usually successful; much of the writing that survives from the early Church Fathers was written as part of the ongoing debate over Christianity. When debate failed, charges of heresy were declared. The views

Nestorius defended were condemned as heresy at the 431 Council of Ephesus, and the Assyrian Church of the East was the first particular church to separate from the young and newly unified community of Catholic churches. The Assyrian Church of the East has continued to teach Nestorian beliefs since, and Nestorians—some of them Assyrian, some Chaldean—have often come under persecution, many of them seeking out refuge and fresh starts as immigrants to the United States. Most of them settled in Chicago.

ISLAM

Judaism, Christianity, and Islam constitute the Abrahamic religions, which have in common their origins with the monotheistic religion of the patriarch Abraham, and their reliance on divine revelation and a prophetic tradition. The Abrahamic group is the largest religious group in the world, including about 3.5 billion followers; the next largest groups are the Dharmic group of Indian religions and the Taoist and Confucian groups of Asian religions. Within the Abrahamic group, Islam is the youngest but second-largest faith, approximately 10 times larger than Judaism. The religion was founded in the 7th century by Muhammad bin 'Abdullāh (570–632), whose prophetic revelations were recorded by his followers in the form of the Qur'an. While

The completion of the Islamic Center in Washington, D.C., in 1957 was a milestone for Muslim Americans, and President Eisenhower joined in the dedication of the building.

A belly dancer in a cabaret in Damascus around 1940, just before the dance spread widely in the United States through the influence of Arab Americans.

Belly Dancing

In Arabic, the folk dance Americans know as belly dancing is called *raqs sharqi*, "oriental dance." The "belly dance" term is a Western one, coined when the dance was demonstrated at the 1899 World's Fair, and reflects the Western shock and titillation over the belly-baring costume worn by dancers, and the gyrations they performed that drew attention to it. Raqs sharqi is a theatrical form, intended for performance, of the simpler dance called *raqs baladi* ("country dance"), which is often danced by the attendees at weddings, festivals, and family reunions. The origins of neither dance are clear, but performers and club owners would often bill the dance as one related to ancient dances of temple priestesses (especially fertility dances, emphasizing the sexual appeal of the dancers) or the Romani ("gypsy") people.

In the 1950s the Arab-American population in New York was large and established enough that a number of Arab nightclubs were opening, becoming a popular part of city life not only for Arab Americans, but also for other ethnic groups. It was at these nightclubs that mainstream America was introduced to belly dancing, performed on stage by hired dancers (many of them Greek or Turkish, or Americans who had learned by watching). Belly dancing spread from the clubs to college campuses and non-Arab homes, and at the same time it became a part of their culture that Arab Americans could feel free to explore without distancing themselves from mainstream American culture.

the Christian Bible incorporates some of the Jewish Scriptures in the form of its Old Testament, the Qur'an stands alone; important material from the Jewish and Christian traditions that is relevant to Islam is retold within the Qur'an from a Muslim perspective.

A Muslim is "one who submits to God," a follower of Islam; Muslim and Islam are derived from the same root word, meaning submission to God. A key Muslim belief, slightly different than most Christian or Jewish views of their own faiths, is that Islam always existed, from Adam on: the revelation imparted to Muhammad did not create a religion, but rather revived and corrected one, while Judaism and Christianity are departures from the original Abrahamic (and Adamic) path. By contrast, Christianity perceives a series of covenants, with different agreements between God and man applicable in different eras. This difference has colored the Abrahamic religions' relationships with one another.

In addition to the Qur'an, Islamic law—sharia—is influenced by the *Hadith* (chronicles of the life of Muhammad) and *ijmaa* (the consensus of the Muslim community), and sharia in turn is interpreted variously by the religious, legal, and bureaucratic institutions of various countries. Just as much of Europe was united by Christendom, with religious reasoning and papal influence forming a significant part of Medieval international law, so too was the Arab world united by Islam.

The Five Pillars of Islam outline the duties expected of every Muslim: the belief in one God and his prophet Muhammad, prayer five times a day, the performance of a pilgrimage to the city of Mecca, fasting during the month of Ramadan, and giving to charity. Prayer is performed facing Mecca, the city where Muhammad introduced Islam, and which tradition holds was founded by descendants of Ishmael, the son of Abraham by his concubine. Further, bodies are expected to be buried facing Mecca, which is one reason early Arab immigrants often arranged for their bodies to be sent back to the home country for burial, until their communities had developed such numbers that Muslim cemeteries could be opened.

Muslim women are not allowed to marry non-Muslim men, and although women are equal before God, they need not be equal before the law. Further, men and women worship separately, an issue for Muslim immigrants around the world as the first mosques established in a new community do not always provide space for women; the public performance of piety is considered the man's role.

DENOMINATIONS OF ISLAM

The two largest denominations of Islam are the Sunni (the largest) and the Shi'a, whose original differences stemmed from disagreement over the question of who should guide Islam after Muhammad's death. The Sunni believe that guidance fell to four caliphs; the Shi'a trace a succession of Imams (religious leaders;

Islam does not have priests in the same sense as other religions) from only one of those caliphs, Muhammad's son-in-law Ali bin Abi Talib. It is generally true that the Shi'a is the less lenient denomination in terms of obedience to Islamic authorities, ascribing its Imams with infallibility, while the Sunni include several different traditions with different interpretations. However, this is a generalization about an old and complex religious tradition, and the application of Muslim law is affected both by denomination and by country. The Shi'a are most prominent in Iran, Iraq, Afghanistan, and Yemen. Although most Arab immigrants are Sunni Muslims, the religious minorities—Muslim and otherwise—have immigrated in greater percentages.

SUEZ CRISIS OF 1956

In the late 1950s, one of the events that further drove a wedge between the Arab world and the West was the Suez Crisis, an attack on Egypt by the combined forces of Israel, Britain, and France—the latter two nations having been involved as imperial powers in the region through much of the 19th and early 20th centuries. The Suez Canal was critical to trade in the region because of its strategic location connecting the Mediterranean to the Red Sea, allowing ships to avoid a long passage around Africa. The canal was critical enough that the West felt it could not let its economic interests be put in jeopardy by the new Egyptian government, which announced its intent to nationalize the canal, putting it directly under government control, when the British and Americans withdrew their offer to finance the construction of the Aswan Dam on the Nile River.

The British used the canal regularly, and had originally laid claim on it in the name of the defense of British India. By 1956 India was independent, but Britain still needed the canal for trade with Australia and New Zealand. Though Britain had a real interest in repairing British-Egyptian relations in the wake of the 1952 revolution, its need for the canal exceeded that interest, and it did not trust the stability of the Egyptian regime or its ability to keep the canal functioning. The Americans largely stayed out of the matter, President Eisenhower wanting to preserve the country's alliance with Saudi Arabia, which was deeply opposed to Britain's relationship with Jordan and Iraq.

But when American attempts at diplomacy consistently failed, the British gathered their allies and seized the canal. It was successfully taken, but fighting persisted, and the American government—simultaneously dealing with the international implications of the Hungarian revolution—feared the possibility of the global East/West, communist/capitalist, conflict that so many awaited in the aftermath of World War II. The Soviet Union and its Warsaw Pact allies spoke of intervening in Egypt's defense, and just as the Vietnam War a decade later would be seen as a conflict that could spiral into World War III, the Suez Crisis seemed to threaten the same. While the United States would refuse to leave Vietnam until the last possible moment, it had not yet committed any military action in the Suez, and demanded a cease-fire, appealing to the United Nations to do the same. An emergency special session of the General Assembly—necessitated by Britain and France's use of their vetoes in the UN Security Council meetings about the matter—found agreement with the American objections, and there was some talk of expelling the countries from the NATO pact if they did not comply. By the weekend, the conflict had ended, Britain and France withdrawing their forces.

UN peacekeepers were placed in the area, both to protect the canal from future invasions, and to ensure the safety of those ships traveling through it. In addition to raising Arab fears of being treated as second-class world citizens—a ground for a proxy war like Southeast Asia, a child to be fought over by Western parents—the Suez Crisis strengthened the perception of Israel as the West's Middle East favorite, and demonstrated the decline of Britain and France's position as world powers when they did not have American support.

CONCLUSION

In the 1950s, the Arab Americans of the second wave were a diverse group, including Druze, Copts, Chaldeans, Nestorians, and a large number of Sunni and Shi'a Muslims. Some of the trends that began in the 1950s would accelerate in the 1960s and beyond, including the growing numbers of immigrants who were fleeing upheavals in the Middle East rather than emigrating for purely economic reasons. The percentage of Muslims among new immigrants increased over the next half-century, reaching 75 percent in the 2000s. It would still be decades, however, before their descendants and new immigrants alike would come to see themselves collectively as "Arab Americans."

BILL KTE'PI
INDEPENDENT SCHOLAR

Further Reading

Abraham, Nabeel, and Sameer Y. Abraham, eds. *Arabs in the New World: Studies on Arab American Communities.* Detroit, MI: Wayne State University Center for Urban Ethnic Studies, 1983.

Aswad, Barbara C., and Barbara Bilge, eds. *Family and Gender Among American Muslims.* Philadelphia, PA: Temple University Press, 1996.

Atiyeh, George, ed. *Arab and American Cultures.* Washington, D.C.: American Enterprise Institute for Public Policy Research, 1977.

Blatty, William Peter. *Which Way to Mecca, Jack?* New York: B. Geis, 1960.

Booshada, Elizabeth. *Arab American Faces and Voices: The Origins of an Immigrant Community.* Austin, TX: University of Texas Press, 2003.

Dimbleby, Jonathan. *The Palestinians*. New York: Quartet Books, 1980.

Elkholy, Abdo A. *The Arab Muslims in the United States: Religion and Assimilation*. New Haven, CT: College and University Press, 1966.

Haddad, Yvonne Yazbeck, and John Esposito, eds. *Muslims on the Americanization Path?* New York: Oxford University Press, 1998.

Hitti, Philip K. *The Arabs: A Short History*. Washington D.C.: Regnery, 1970.

Lunde, Paul. *Islam: Faith, Culture, History*. New York: Dorling Kindersley, 2002.

Marschner, Janice. *California's Arab Americans*. Sacramento, CA: Coleman Ranch, 2003.

Naff, Alixia. *The Arab Americans*. New York: Chelsea House, 1988.

Orfalea, Gregory. *The Arab Americans*. Northampton, MA: Olive Branch Press, 2006.

Suleiman, Michael, ed. *Arabs in America: Building a New Future*. Philadelphia, PA: Temple University Press, 1999.

Wolfe, Michael. *Taking Back Islam: American Muslims Reclaim Their Faith*. Emmaus, PA: Rodale, 2002.

CHAPTER 6

The Sixties: 1960 to 1969

THE 1960s SAW the end of the second wave of Arab immigration and the beginning of the third wave (from 1967 to the present). It was a time when the second wave immigrants were beginning to settle in, when young Arab Americans struggled with their identity and place in a youth-centric culture, and a time of social upheaval around the world. Even more than in previous decades, in the 1960s the Middle East was a politically volatile place, and a number of significant political and cultural world events affected not only patterns of Arab immigration, but also the lives and attitudes of established Arab Americans.

CHANGES IN IMMIGRATION LAWS

The Immigration and Nationality Act of 1965 was, from a demographic standpoint and in light of its long-term cultural implications, one of the most important pieces of American legislation ever passed. It abandoned the race- and nationality-based quotas of previous immigration legislation, which had limited the annual number of immigrants from any given country. The only limits were placed according to hemisphere—120,000 a year from the Western Hemisphere, 170,000 from the Eastern Hemisphere, and no more than 20,000 immigrants from any one country. Family members of existing U.S. residents did not count toward these quotas; thus, a man could immigrate to

Arab-Israeli Six Day War of 1967

Having initially seized most of the former state of Palestine in 1948 when Arab forces attacked it, Israel expanded its borders again in 1967, occupying Egypt's Sinai Peninsula, as well as seizing territories that had been controlled by non-Palestinian Arab powers since 1948: the Gaza Strip, the West Bank, and the Golan Heights. Israel's Arab opponents (Egypt, Jordan, and Syria primarily, with assistance contributed by Algeria, Iraq, Morocco, Saudi Arabia, the Sudan, and Tunisia) were unable to defeat the smaller state, which had the result of strengthening both Israel's confidence and Arab sentiment against it. The war, though it had many contributing factors, was directly precipitated by a lie concocted by the Soviet Union, which informed Arab leaders that the Israeli Army was preparing to invade Syria. This led Egyptian President Nasser to force the UN peacekeeping force out of the Sinai Peninsula, which it had been occupying since the 1957 Suez Crisis. All of this speaks to the Arab/Israeli conflict's context in the Cold War, at a time when wars were being fought in Southeast Asia in the name of the great communist/capitalist divide.

The war tripled Israel's territory and put one million non-Jewish Arabs under its rule. Though it lasted only a week, it was one of the most significant political events of the decade—and of the second half of the 20th century. The war is generally considered the first significant moment in the development of Arab political consciousness since the creation of Israel, and as such resonated with Arabs throughout the world.

the United States in one year, and fly the rest of his family out to join him with no fear of a quota problem.

The impact of the Immigration and Nationality Act has been significant, permanently changing the ethnic makeup of the United States. Immigration doubled from 1965 to 1970. In non-European countries, the change has been the most pronounced. Prospective Arab immigrants found the United States a much more feasible destination than in the past, and many who might have otherwise settled in Europe or Canada came to the United States, with its room to spare and ample economic opportunities. In addition to family reunification visas, immigration law privileged skilled workers and refugees, further accounting for some of the immigration to the United States from the Arab world.

THE THIRD WAVE OF ARAB IMMIGRATION TO THE UNITED STATES

A third wave of Arab immigration began in 1967. Unlike the second wave, which came after a lull in immigration, the third wave began immediately after the second, but is categorized separately. While most second wave immigrants were Egyptian (as most first wave immigrants had been Syrian), most of the third wave immigrants were Palestinian, though their country of origin was more often listed as Jordan, a stop along the way.

In the 1950s and 1960s, political turmoil in the Middle East and subsequent immigration to the United States resulted in the critical "brain drain" of the region, as more and more of those leaving their Arab countries were well educated professionals. By 1983 half of those with Ph.D.s were leaving the Arab world behind, a startlingly high figure and one that indicates a particular characteristic of the third wave. These immigrants were even more likely to be professionals than the second wave, who were well-educated, highly skilled, and often prosperous. While many immigrants in the past came to the United States for greater economic advantages, some of the third wave actually found themselves worse off financially after immigrating, unable to make a lateral career move because of a lack of connections, or because American employers did not value foreign experience.

One of the increasingly prominent factors in Arab immigration was the rise of Islamic fundamentalism, which made sects like the Egyptian Copts and the Iraqi Chaldeans feel out of place or unwelcome in their home countries. The Chaldean and Copt populations in the United States continued to rise after the 1960s as a result, especially after the ascension of the Ba'ath Party in Iraq. Chaldeans tended to settle in Detroit, adding to the growing Arab community there; Copts settled in large numbers in Jersey City.

THE NORTH YEMEN CIVIL WAR

Most Yemeni Americans first immigrated to the United States during the civil war fought in North Yemen from 1962 to 1970. In 1962 a coup dethroned Imam Muhammad al-Badr a week after he was crowned king of North Yemen upon the death of his father. The revolutionary forces were inspired by the pan-Arab nationalism espoused by Gamal Abdul Nasser, the Egyptian president whose regime had already alienated so many of the Copts who immigrated to the United States. The coup was led by the commander of the royal guard, Abdullah as-Sallal, who declared himself president. Al-Badr fled and was declared dead by the revolutionaries, but survived to lead the royalist forces in an attempt to reclaim his kingdom. The war was bloody and lasted for the remainder of the decade. Though al-Badr was successful in regaining much of the territory of North Yemen, Saudi Arabia—his main ally along with the British—recognized the legitimacy of the revolutionary government in 1970, shocking al-Badr and effectively ending his rule.

North and South Yemen had been governed separately for generations, the area of South Yemen having been bound together as the Aden Protectorate under 19th-century British rule and considered part of British India until 1937, at which point it was managed directly as a crown colony. Because of the turmoil in North Yemen, the British attempted to force all of the Aden Protectorate states into a Federation of Arab Emirates of the South in the 1960s, an attempt that backfired by increasing anti-British sentiments in the region. The National Liberation Front was formed to attempt to force the British out of the region, and when the situation and safety of British citizens had deteriorated enough and the Suez Canal was temporarily closed in 1967, the British finally withdrew. Left to its own devices, Aden became the People's Republic of South Yemen, a socialist state that converted to stricter communism when the Marxist wing of the NLF took power in the summer of 1969.

YEMENI IMMIGRATION

Most of the Yemeni who came to the United States after the war came not from communist southern Yemen but from capitalist North Yemen—the largest share coming from Ash-Shaar, a border town that took the brunt of the war's violence. The Yemeni coming from communist Yemen were significantly better-educated as a group than their northern countrymen, having much in common with the third wave Arab immigrants fleeing uncomfortable political regimes. The northern Yemeni were more often rural, working class, or poor, and their immigration was often funded by the *wakil al-mughtaribin*— moneylenders based in northern Yemen and operating according to the rules of Islamic banking, which prohibits the collection of interest as a form of usury. Instead, the wakil are paid with *qahwa*—literally, "coffee money," flat payments made as thanks for the loan. Typically, the arrangement was for the wakil to finance a Yemeni immigrant's move to the United States, providing money for moving expenses, plane fare, and even living expenses for the family staying behind; the Yemeni would take an American job, often arranged by a countryman who had already settled in the area.

It was in the best interest of the wakil to maintain a list of such contacts, and the influx of American dollars was beneficial to the Yemeni economy as a whole. After paying for his own modest expenses in the United States, the Yemeni would send the rest of his paycheck to the wakil, who would take his coffee money and a portion for repayment of the loan before distributing the rest of the balance to the worker's family. Because of the disparity between the cost of living in the two countries and the strength of the U.S. dollar, a modestly living Yemeni could afford a prosperous lifestyle for his family back home, even on laborer's wages. Quite often, two-thirds of the worker's paycheck would be sent home. As with many other immigrant groups, Yemeni were known for their willingness to work long hours, weekends, and holidays.

Many Yemeni immigrants took farm jobs in California, or factory jobs in industrial midwest cities like Detroit and Canton. Yemeni Americans constituted a distinct and remarkable group of Arab Americans. In contrast with most of the second and third wave immigrants, 90 percent of Yemeni immigrants were young men without families, or with families back home. Few were fully literate or fluent in English, and they were less likely than other groups to pick up significant English fluency once in the country. As a group, Yemeni Americans often did not settle down in the United States at all, but rather commuted back and forth between the two countries, using the money earned in the United States to pay for expenses for themselves and their families in Yemen, often traveling back home several times a year.

Because so many of the Yemeni continued to use Arabic, their neighborhoods were often as full of Arabic-language signage as Chinatowns were of Chinese-language advertisements. This was especially the case in the South End of Dearborn, Michi-

A Yemeni-American mother in traditional dress with her daughter in Lackawanna, New York.

gan, a Detroit suburb, which beginning in the 1960s enjoyed the densest Arab population in the United States, thanks to an influx of Yemeni immigrants settling in a neighborhood already heavily inhabited by Lebanese. Like the various Chinatowns, Arab communities like the South End became as much language communities as ethnic communities, places where residents were surrounded by people of their own language, newspapers they could read, and a cultural support group. By the end of the century, half of the South End would become Yemeni-owned, but the rise started in the 1960s.

The Yemeni Americans' hardworking lifestyle naturally led to less integration or assimilation than among other groups, and a different attitude toward such integration, without the explicit prohibition against integration as might be found in communities such as the Hasidic Jews or the Amish. In Yemeni-American communities, the homeless and out of work were called *bumin*, roughly, slang for "bums;" to avoid work was one of the greatest social sins for Yemeni-Americans. However, some Yemeni young men arriving in the United States were overwhelmed by the vices available to them. Giving in to the temptations of alcohol, gambling, or the loosening sexual mores of the 1960s, they were quickly dubbed *ta`ishin*, "slackers." Contact with mainstream, urban-American society was seen as fraught with risk of becoming ta`ishin. Such contact was rare in the 1960s, except among the occasional young man taking an American girl on a casual date, or from an American-born second-generation Yemeni American

Young Yemeni-American men at work in a grocery store in New York. In the 1960s, 90 percent of Yemenis in the United States were single men or men who immigrated without their families.

brought up in American schools—but they represented a tiny fraction of the total Yemeni-American population in the second wave and early third wave years. The lack of contact often extended to voluntary disenfranchisement; in the 1960s and for years afterward, few Yemeni Americans voted in American elections, at the local, state, or federal level. The reason was apparently not a lack of access or awareness, but rather a lack of interest.

THE PUBLIC AND PRIVATE WORLDS OF ARAB-AMERICAN FAMILIES

More than most ethnic groups, many Arab Americans in the 1960s struck a balance between assimilation and isolation by drawing a line between the public "American" world and the private "Arab" world, in which there were different norms of behavior in different spheres. In the public world, Arab Americans worked in a predominantly non-Arab environment, in which their

What Is Acceptable to Eat

Halal is an Arabic term meaning "permissible." In the Muslim diaspora, it refers to food that is acceptable to eat under Muslim laws concerning food and diet. In this sense it is similar to the Jewish term kosher. The Qur'an forbids the consumption of alcohol (and by extension, drugs), pork, carrion, blood, animals killed by certain means, and food that has not been prayed over. Animals other than seafood are to be killed by ritual slaughter, which severs the jugular veins and carotid arteries on both sides of the neck, without harming the spinal cord.

There are many concerns about adhering to halal restrictions when living in a non-Muslim country. Meat prepared by a halal butcher is not available outside of some communities with high Muslim populations. In a restaurant, even ordering chicken may result in some cross-contamination with pork or other forbidden substances. Alcohol is present in a great many items, not only in wine or liquor added to a sauce, but in the form of flavor extracts such as the vanilla used in cakes. In the 1960s, as in the decades earlier, there was an ongoing discussion in the Muslim world about whether or not Coca-Cola's secret formula involved any alcohol-based extracts; while the alcohol content was minimal enough to be unnoticed and acceptable by government agency standards, religious standards were much stricter.

In the 1960s, the food industry was not as open as it would be in later decades. Inquiring about the ingredients of a restaurant dish risked an inaccurate answer, or no answer at all. Although grocery food labels were required to list ingredients, they gave no indication of whether, for instance, pig enzymes and alcohol were used in additives. Many American Muslims rely on kosher butchers, which are more common than halal butchers. There is no universal consensus on whether kosher butchering standards satisfy halal requirements, but kosher meat is closer to halal meat than non-kosher meat.

In the 1960s Muslims struggled with a secretive U.S. food industry and a lack of halal butchers.

ethnicity was irrelevant, neither drawn upon nor denied. In the suburbs, the private world usually included the home, and perhaps a local Arab American mosque, church, or social club. In urban Arab-American neighborhoods, the "private" world sometimes extended to include part of the local community. Either way, in the private world, Arab norms were more strongly in effect, governing family dynamics. Sometimes Arabic was spoken in the home, although the children, except in some rare cases, were also fluent in English.

Mothers were the primary caretakers of children; when a child (or an adult) misbehaved, it reflected more strongly on his mother than on his father. Mothers taught the children the things that were expected of them, and were responsible for most of the discipline in the household. Fathers were authority figures, and assumed a disciplinary role if the child's wrongdoing was severe, if there was a pattern of behavioral problems, or if the child consistently disrespected his mother. As in many households, punishment from the father was more feared because he was a more impersonal figure, seen less often because he spent more time at work and away from the family; the very rareness of his discipline made it more effective.

Chronic problems such as alcoholism, an apparent lack of ethics or values, gambling, drug addictions, or womanizing reflected on the family. Like many communities, Arab-American communities were prone to gossip, which was defended on the grounds that it reinforced shared values. In sharp contrast to urban neighborhoods and apartment buildings where neighbors may not even know each others' names, in the Arab-American community, the gossip grapevine allowed a parent to find out if a child had been seen smoking in the alley, if a girl had developed a "reputation," if a boy had been skipping school, or if teenagers attended a party where alcohol was served. In 1960s Muslim communities, even young people of legal drinking age were discouraged from attending parties with alcohol, which were seen as one of the temptations of the secular American world. Children knew that anything they were seen doing would make it back to the parents; parents in turn knew that there were few secrets that could be kept in the home, and that they would be judged according to their children's behavior, which motivated them to keep from shirking their parental duties.

EDUCATION AND AMERICANIZATION

All of this contributed to a distrust of the American public school system, particularly in areas that did not have a long history of Arab-American presence, and which therefore did not have a predominantly Arab-American student or faculty population. Like many immigrant groups, Arab-American parents saw the public school system as a force that eroded cultural traditions through homogenization. What Arab American parents saw as homogenization, education policy makers called uniformity, and uniformity of public education was an American goal through most of the 20th century. Uniformity ensured a common standard throughout schools, so that graduates from any high school could be expected to have comparable educations, encouraging colleges to compare transcripts and standardized test results. Combined with the social effects of mixing adolescents together for the greater part of the day, a general uniformity of curriculum naturally led to a degree of homogenization. Even when teachers were sensitive to the concerns of immigrant or second-generation American parents, this was a difficult process to prevent, and in the 1960s most teachers saw Americanization as a goal parents should want for their children.

Arab-American teenagers typically faced earlier curfews than their classmates. While spanking was fairly common in the 1960s across all ethnic groups, corporal punishment was used on Arab-American children through a later age than was typical of American children, even through the end of the teens. Babysitters were rarely used; older children cared for younger children, and younger children were expected to learn to behave very quickly, certainly by the time they were in elementary school. Parents expected to have a say in their children's lives even later in life when the children were grown and living outside the house, though there was an understanding that a married daughter had joined her husband's family, and was perhaps under their "jurisdiction."

DATING AND GENDER ROLES

In the 1960s the traditional American ideals of individualism and independence naturally led to an increasing number of unmarried young people moving out of their parents' homes. However, often young men and women moved in together, whether as part of a sexual relationship or simply as roommates, and the Arab-American's expectation of young people's behavior was increasingly at odds with the mainstream. Sometimes this encouraged young Arab Americans to remain close to their community, where they were surrounded by people governed by the same norms. In other instances, especially in the suburbs where Arab Americans attended school with American children from all heritages, it emphasized the generation gap that teenagers all across the country were feeling. Sometimes confronting that gap led parents to loosen their requirements a little, to seek a middle ground that didn't compromise their values; at other times, they simply increased their punishments or watched their children more closely for infractions and wrongdoing. A large proportion of Arab-American teenagers, especially with second or third wave parents, attended college, which increased their exposure to the non-Arab world.

Just as Arab-American adults in the public world interacted with non-Arabs, so too did Arab-American children in school and after school. Arab-American boys were usually allowed to date non-Arab girls; Arab-American girls, however, were not allowed to date non-Arab boys, and Muslim girls in particular were traditionally forbidden from dating non-Muslim boys. The relationship

Strict rules and traditional values could become a source of conflict between generations in Arab-American families, especially for girls whose upbringing contrasted so starkly with the spread of feminism in American culture in the 1960s.

between siblings was an important part of the family dynamic, especially between brothers and sisters. Brothers were essentially peer-chaperones to their sisters, and responsible for protecting their reputation. Sisters took on a motherly role—advisory, not disciplinary—sometimes settling disputes between young siblings. The closeness of siblings, and often cousins, persisted long after marriage, and it was common for Arab immigrants to settle in places where their brothers, cousins, or uncles had already found a home.

Girls were expected to contribute to household chores more than boys, reflecting the expectations that would be put on them in adulthood. The dating lives of girls were also much more closely monitored. In the 1960s it was still common for some Arab-American girls to be forbidden from dating at all, restricting their interaction with the opposite sex to chaperoned parties and school functions, a constant source of friction between daughters and parents. While boys were thus the most likely to become somewhat Americanized or homogenized, because the norms of their behavior most closely resembled their classmates and because they had the most intimate interaction with non-Arabs, Arab-American girls born and raised in the United States were most likely to express resentment of their heritage. This was particularly true given the rise of feminism in mainstream America, a topic of discussion in American schools. Both boys and girls, of course, faced mockery and ostracism at school for anything that set them apart—the food they brought for lunch, the clothes they wore, the color of their skin, their names, or the restrictions of family life. There was a natural desire among most adolescent Arab Americans to minimize their differences, at least in public.

The elderly were traditionally cared for by their family—in the 1960s, Arab Americans did not yet accept the American institution of retirement homes or managed care, except in rare cases where constant medical attention was required.

AFRICAN-AMERICAN MUSLIMS

Throughout most of American history, Islam was a religion of immigrants, something brought into the country from outside. There were few converts, and unlike Buddhism, another religion foreign to American shores, white Americans rarely delved into Islam to explore its teachings—though the mystical Muslim sect of Sufism enjoyed occasional attention on college campuses. The rise of black Muslims—African-Americans converting to Islam, a move often strongly associated with black power, ethnic pride, and the civil rights movement—changed that, putting American Muslims in the spotlight of the nightly news and the weekly magazines.

The Nation of Islam was founded in 1930 in Detroit by Wallace Dodd Ford, who changed his name to Wallace Fard Muhammad. His origins are unclear, but some reports place him from New Zealand (the official Nation of Islam position is that he was an Arab from Mecca, and furthermore that he was God in human form). Fard espoused the belief that the white race was "the devil," while blacks were a chosen people, beloved by God. The Nation of Islam combined traditional Muslim teachings and a call for ethnic pride among African Americans with mystical teachings such as theosophy that had circulated since the 19th century. That connection to esoteric mystical cults may have been connected to the ritual murder committed by one of Fard's followers; Fard was arrested for his involvement in 1934. He then handed over leadership of the Nation of Islam to one of his earliest converts, Elijah Muhammad, formerly Elijah Poole. Elijah led the organization until 1975, but it was Malcolm X who became its public face.

The Ba'ath Party and Arab Socialism

The Arab Socialist Ba'ath Party was the first secular pan-Arab movement, founded during World War II by Syrian schoolteacher Michel Aflaq, with an eye toward the Arab world's need for unity in the aftermath of the war and the long-awaited recession of European colonial influences. The name of the party, the Arabic word for "resurrection," came from Aflaq's essay *On the Way of Resurrection,* a word he used to refer to a pan-Arab Renaissance. The goal of the Ba'ath party was to resist and repel Western colonial rule, to encourage pan-Arab cooperation and eventual unity, and to promote what has become known as Arab socialism.

While European socialism is secular, even anti-religious in cases where the old European religious institutions are wrested of power, and where it often seeks to dismantle nationalist traditions, Arab socialism is strongly nationalist and strongly spiritual. While it need not specifically be Muslim, and generally seeks to overcome the problems of religious conflicts between denominations or between faiths, Arab socialism respects the Muslim traditions of the Arab world and attempts to keep them intact. Aflaq in particular vocally rejected traditional Marxism and its atheist foundations. Thus, greater rights for women, for instance, are fought for within a Muslim-friendly context, rather than by attempting to divorce the culture from Islam. Outside the actions of the Ba'ath Party, the main gains of Arab socialism in the postwar years were the land reforms in Egypt and Syria that greatly improved the lots of the lower and working classes, and removed much of the privilege and exploitative power of the major landowners. Major industries and the banking system were also nationalized. Arab socialism was often characterized as a middle ground between Western capitalism and Eastern communism, though this was somewhat of a simplification.

After some years as a party with varying levels of influence in different Arab countries, the Ba'ath Party came to power in both Syria and Iraq in 1963, and remained in control of Syria. Though power in Iraq was held for only a few months, it was regained in 1968 and remained in power until being banned by the Coalition Provisional Authority in 2003. The sudden acquisition of power shook up the Ba'ath Party, and the party underwent a coup that took Aflaq out of power. The factional struggles within the party and the subsequent power shifts as it took control were some of the factors that led Arabs to leave the country for new homes.

Malcolm X had converted to the Nation of Islam while in prison, and through the 1950s became an increasingly visible and controversial face in the civil rights movement. In the 1960s Malcolm X was responsible for convincing black heavyweight champion boxer Cassius Clay to convert to the Nation of Islam, changing his name to Muhammad Ali in the process. It was the sin-

Muhammad Ali (seated at upper left) listens to an address by Nation of Islam leader Elijah Muhammad in 1964. Ali took on his Islamic name that year.

gle action that brought more attention to American Muslims than any other. Soon after, Malcolm left the Nation of Islam and became a part of mainstream Sunni Islam, making a pilgrimage to Mecca; Ali eventually did likewise. The conversion made Ali a political figure, as well as one of the most popular and successful athletes of his generation and in the history of his sport. When news sources sought him out for a sound-bite reaction to the major events of the day, the views he espoused—like other members of the Nation of Islam and some members of the black nationalist movement in general—sometimes went beyond the goals of the civil rights movement toward separatism, the segregation of black and white cultures. He declared himself a conscientious objector of the Vietnam War, both because of his religious beliefs and because of his race, adding, "I ain't got no quarrel with them Viet Cong—they never called me nigger." He was found guilty of refusing to be drafted into the armed forces, a conviction the Supreme Court later overturned in 1971.

Not all African-American Muslims were so controversial or separatist, nor did all share the Nation of Islam's belief in black supremacy. Malcolm X's conversion to Sunni Islam—likely a contributing factor in his assassination—was one of many, as groups like the Nation of Islam created interest in Islam for African Americans, who eventually sought elsewhere for more information about the religion. But the effect on Arab Americans was confusing. Suddenly, many of the most prominent Americans on television with Arabic names were African Americans who had chosen those names themselves; American Muslims were a topic of interest in the news, and yet reporters covered more African Americans converting to new Islamic splinter groups rather than the men and women who had been attending mosques in American cities for decades. Although the intersection of Islam and black nationalism often referred to the population of Muslim African slaves, Arab Americans nevertheless felt that something of their identity had been poached and borrowed, and it made many of them uneasy—not to mention the necessity of sometimes distancing their mainstream mosques from the Nation of Islam.

ARAB AMERICANS AND RACE

The American conception of race has historically not made room for Arab Americans. Originally classified as white beginning with the 1960 U.S. Census, Arab Americans were allowed to identify themselves as they pleased. But because of that linguistic history, there was a clear divide between Arab Americans and the non-whites whose explorations, defenses, and reclamations of their ethnic pride led to various social movements in the 1950s and beyond. They weren't "black" like African Americans, "yellow" as Asian Americans had derisively been called in the past, or the "brown" of Latin Americans. At the same time, it seemed strange to call "white" both a Lebanese factory worker and the Anglo American who owned the factory. This quasi-whiteness contributed to Arab-American communities forming barrier populations in many parts of the country where they were densely settled, such as Chicago—neighborhoods that separated white communities from African-American communities. Arab Americans can have a wide range of skin tones, due to to various ethnic groups in their collective background. In the 1960s they challenged and defied conventional American expectations of race.

CONCLUSION

The civil rights movement of the 1960s helped to prompt self-definition and politicize issues of race and collective ethnic identity. In the wake of the Six Days War and the coverage in the American media, with Arabs increasingly portrayed as villains and aggressors—far from the romantic Sheikh or other positive media images—Arab Americans began to identify as Arabs, rather than simply Lebanese, Egyptian, or Palestinian. Like the other ethnic pride movements of the era, it was a way to reclaim and reframe an ethnic identity rather than to downplay or hide from it. Additionally, they were not simply Arabs, they were Arab *Americans*—as much as German Americans, Irish Americans, or any other Americans. As American awareness of the Middle

East grew, and as events in the Middle East rose to the fore on the international stage, this shared identity became more important among Arab Americans, regardless of country of origin. This did not lead to a pan-Arab American community; differences in heritage were still present, such as the difference between Muslims and Christians, Shi'a and Sunni, and refugees from right-wing and left-wing regimes. But ironically, those differences were also important because the mainstream media's perception that all Arabs were the same factored in spurring on this rise in collective identity in the 1960s.

BILL KTE'PI
INDEPENDENT SCHOLAR

Further Reading

Abraham, Nabeel and Sameer Y. Abraham, eds. *Arabs in the New World: Studies on Arab American Communities*. Detroit, MI: Wayne State University Center for Urban Ethnic Studies, 1983.

Aswad, Barbara C. and Barbara Bilge, eds. *Family and Gender Among American Muslims*. Philadelphia, PA: Temple University Press, 1996.

Atiyeh, George, ed. *Arab and American Cultures*. Washington, D.C.: American Enterprise Institute for Public Policy Research, 1977.

Blatty, William Peter. *Which Way to Mecca, Jack?* New York: B. Geis, 1960.

Booshada, Elizabeth. *Arab American Faces and Voices: The Origins of an Immigrant Community*. Austin, TX: University of Texas Press, 2003.

Daniels, Roger. *Guarding the Golden Door: American Immigration Policy and Immigrants Since 1882*. New York: Hill and Wang, 2004.

Dimbleby, Jonathan. *The Palestinians*. New York: Quartet Books, 1980.

Elkholy, Abdo A. *The Arab Muslims in the United States: Religion and Assimilation*. New Haven, CT: College and University Press, 1966.

Haddad, Yvonne Yazbeck and John Esposito, eds. *Muslims on the Americanization Path?* New York: Oxford University Press, 1998.

Hitti, Philip K. *The Arabs: A Short History*. Washington, D.C.: Regnery, 1970.

Lunde, Paul. *Islam: Faith, Culture, History*. New York: Dorling Kindersley, 2002.

Marschner, Janice. *California's Arab Americans*. Sacramento, CA: Coleman Ranch, 2003.

Naff, Alixia. *The Arab Americans*. New York: Chelsea House, 1988.

Orfalea, Gregory. *The Arab Americans*. Northampton, MA: Olive Branch Press, 2006.

Suleiman, Michael, ed. *Arabs in America: Building a New Future*. Philadelphia, PA: Temple University Press, 1999.

Wolfe, Michael. *Taking Back Islam: American Muslims Reclaim Their Faith*. Emmaus, PA: Rodale, 2002.

CHAPTER 7

The Seventies: 1970 to 1979

SINCE THE PASSAGE of the U.S. Immigration Act of 1965, which abolished the use of national-origin quotas, more than 400,000 Arabs have arrived in America—among them some of the Arab elite, who came to take advantage of new policies that gave preference to immigrants with professional skills. The reasons for this new migration, which is often referred to as the third wave, differ markedly from those of earlier periods. While economic objectives remain a major cause for migration, a number of related political factors have intermingled to increase the immigration of all Arab nationalities during this period. Political and social instability resulting from coup d'état, revolution, war, and military occupation appear to have accelerated the economic push-pull forces at work.

PUSH-PULL FACTORS IN THE THIRD WAVE
Third wave immigrants arrived from a variety of countries and included Palestinians, Jordanians, Egyptians, Lebanese, Yemenis, and Iraqis. While a large number of Arab migrants were secularists, increasing numbers of devout Muslims arrived in the 1970s, including university students, intellectuals, and professionals. Muslim Arabs arriving since the 1970s have conflicted with the generations of Muslim Arab Americans who laid the foundation of Islamic worship in America. Among Muslim immigrants there was much anxiety and insecurity

about their Islamic identity, often expressed in ways that were restrictive about women's role in society. Many recently imported *imams,* or Muslim leaders, from the Middle East were unfamiliar with American culture and claimed that American Islam must be made to conform to pure Islam as it was practiced in most Arab countries. Rather than accommodating American mores, these newcomers wished to maintain a lifestyle consistent with their understanding of Islam. An increasing number of Islamic religious schools, or *madrassas,* were established to teach young Muslims about their faith. Children could attain both a religious and secular education, similar to a Catholic parochial school.

Over time Muslims won concessions at a number of private and public schools across the United States that helped not only to maintain their Muslim identity, but also to teach it to their children. Several schools and univer-

Brain Drain

Since 1967, economic policies and wars have encouraged a cross-section of Arabs to emigrate. In the last 40 years, Arab countries have experienced major political upheavals that have acted as propelling mechanisms for emigration. A good number of these immigrants came to the United States for post-graduate education or for career reasons, never expecting to return. The number of university graduates increased in the 1970s, but the number of jobs available in their countries did not correspond with their skill level. With few job prospects, many saw immigration as their only option of career advancement, and so they left, contributing to the serious problem in the development of the Arab world that is called the "brain drain."

The graduate educational opportunities available in the United States provided one of the incentives for many bright young Arabs to immigrate. Although Arab universities had good facilities, U.S. schools offered superior academic programs, equipped with the latest technology for medicine and engineering. Therefore, wealthier parents sent their children to the United States for undergraduate or graduate schools. Arab governments and U.S. institutions such as AMIDEAST also helped to facilitate the training of professionals in the United States, believing that they would return to their home countries, skilled and ready to contribute to their society and economy. But the corruption, stagnated economies, flat job market, and poor financial prospects back home forced many to rethink the concept of returning after their schooling was completed. Although some did return, many stayed in the United States where educational opportunities developed into career networks and employment options. These skilled laborers and educated professionals established permanent residency because the lifestyle was better, and income was significantly higher, than what would be possible back home.

sities began to serve halal foods, and public schools no longer required Muslim students to be in the cafeteria at mealtimes during Ramadan, making it easier for them to observe the fast during their holy month.

The major reason for Arab immigration during this period was the two Arab-Israeli wars—in 1967 and 1973—along with the booming oil economies for the Middle East, which had a dra-

Arab Americans protesting in Detroit in the 1970s on behalf of the Palestinians.

matic and far-reaching effect throughout the region and the world. These and other events acted to push immigrants from each nationality group to participate in the largest Arab immigration wave ever to American cities, especially to Detroit, Chicago, New York, and Los Angeles. For the Palestinians, for example, the Israeli military occupation after 1967 produced a new set of political, economic, and social forces within the West Bank–Gaza population, forcing villagers to quit their lands and homes and travel to other countries in search of education, work, and security. While the majority of Palestinians immigrated to nearby Arab countries, a growing number of Palestinians reunited with kinsmen in the United States. Included in the over 37,000 Arab professionals who immigrated to the United States were many Palestinian refugees and Egyptians disillusioned with economic reforms under President Gamal Nasser.

The Lebanese population during the 1975–76 civil wars faced a similar set of forces, particularly in southern Lebanon, which prompted a massive emigration. Already economically underdeveloped through decades of neglect and Israeli invasions, southern Lebanon became a battleground. The chain of events that followed produced a major immigrant influx to the United States and other countries of the world. The continuing border skirmishes between Israeli and Palestinian forces forced many Lebanese to flee to other countries, including the United States. Since the Muslims were the largest group of this third wave of Arab immigrants, they began to fulfill their religious duties without fear of perdition, and building mosques in their neighborhoods.

MUSLIM ARAB-AMERICAN IDENTITIES

For Muslims, any uncontaminated place at home or work could be a place to pray. Both Muslim and Druze immigrants could compensate for the lack of consecrated religious institutions by gathering for prayer, reading from holy books, discussing religion, or celebrating religious festivals.

Historically, the mosque functioned as a gathering place for the community, where Muslims expressed their religious and political allegiance during

The Third-Wave Rush

The spike in immigration after 1965 is often referred to as the third wave of immigration. Many third-wave immigrants were professionals; if anything, the trend intensified. There were differences, however, between the third wave of immigrants and the previous wave. First, and most obvious, was that the third wave was three times larger than the previous wave, largely due to the loosening of U.S. immigration restrictions in 1965. Second, the third wave was fleeing not only intensified Israeli-Arab struggles but also intra-Arab warfare on a scale not seen since the mid-19th century. Lebanese, Iraqi, and Syrian immigrants, for instance, were not just leaving situations that had been shaken by change of rule or new economic structures, as in Nasser's Egypt. They were leaving societies wracked by abysmal violence.

The contemporary Lebanese constituted one of the largest groups of Arab immigrants from the third wave. Iraqis began for the first time to come to the United States in sizeable numbers (over 40,000 after 1967); some of this influx was due to professionals who did not want to fight what they felt was a meaningless war of attrition with Khomeini's Iran, a war that by its sixth year had caused over a million casualties. Syria's prospering economy was beginning to plunge by the mid-1980s, and it contributed sizable numbers of third-wave immigrants. Some of these Syrians were disillusioned by corruption or by the occasional brutality of the Assad regime, whose crushing of Islamic fundamentalist rebels at Hama in 1982 caused the death of perhaps 20,000 civilians. Certain Christian sects, such as the Iraqi Chaldeans and Egyptian Copts, felt increasingly isolated in their societies, and with beachheads already established by a handful of earlier immigrants to America, they also began coming in larger numbers.

the Friday service. In the new country, it acquired a social and cultural meaning as Arab Muslims struggled to maintain an Arab and Islamic identity in an alien culture. Not only were weddings and funerals conducted at the mosque, in keeping with American practices, but even fundraising activities such as mosque bazaars, bake sales, community dinners, and cultural events were adopted. Women participated in other aspects of mosque life generally not open to them in the Middle East. These included attending the Sunday service and teaching Sunday schools. This role was curtailed in areas where more recently arrived immigrants predominated. Coalitions formed between illiterate, traditional rural men and highly educated young students or immigrants committed to a strict Islamic order.

Since the beginning of the 1970s, there has been a return to normative Islam, sometimes referred to as reform and thus retaining a rich cultural legacy. The spike in the U.S. Muslim population encouraged followers who wanted to celebrate and remembered a time when Muslim holidays were virtually ignored. The celebrations in the mosques and organizations added a growing sense of dignity, identity, and purpose for Muslims. The affirmation reflected the growing belief of Muslims that they had a purpose and a message for mankind. The sense of mission in the United States was nurtured by Muslim scholars from India, Pakistan, and Saudi Arabia, who traveled throughout the country proclaiming normative Islam, and by various local organizations that were are committed to *daawah* (mission) and supported by mission funds from Saudi Arabia, Kuwait, Qatar, Libya, and Pakistan. However, Islam did not have an easy task in the United States. Even among immigrant Muslims, mosque participation was limited. Arab Muslims reflected the political, ideological, and territorial differences of the countries from which they emigrated. These differences sometimes became a major focus of contention among individuals affirming exclusive claims to their views of the true Islam. By 1979 there were more than 250 mosques throughout the country, mostly in large metropolitan areas.

CLUBS, SOCIETIES, AND SOLIDARITY

In addition to the attempts to retain their cultural identity through religious institutions, Arab Americans prevailed in the Arabic-language press and in the formation of clubs and societies. In the United States many Syrians learned to organize around a common purpose or cause. They developed such

Among the wide variety of Arab-American academic, social, and business clubs and associations was this soccer team in New York State photographed in the late 1970s.

a propensity for it that at any given time the number of organizations was out of proportion to the number of Syrians in the United States. Family, religious, and village social clubs proliferated in part to counter the rate of mixed marriages and to maintain the continuity of the subgroup. If these clubs had a central and common theme, it was the underlying one of group solidarity mainly through in-group marriage. They tended, therefore, to be exclusivist. Attempts by U.S.-born Syrians to change this divisive custom succeeded only after World War II. However, the Arab-American community continued to feel harassed and threatened, and the often indiscriminate attacks or public displays of hatred for Arabs and Arab Americans during and after the 1967 Arab-Israeli War galvanized Arab Americans to organize in order to fend off discrimination and aggression.

The Arab community in the United States organized the Association of Arab-American University Graduates (AAUG), founded in 1967, which was the first Arab-American organization with political-scholarly goals. The National Association of Arab Americans (NAAA) was founded in 1972. Its goal was to act as a political lobby in Washington on behalf of Arab issues. The first organization to systematically focus on discrimination against Arabs in America was the American-Arab Anti-Discrimination Committee (ADC). As for historical work in this period, one example came from the Institute of Texan Cultures at the University of Texas at San Antonio, which documented the contributions of Syrian and Lebanese Texans to the state's heritage in a 1974 collection. A richly printed booklet includes stories and photographs of early Arab-American settlers at social gatherings, family functions, church meetings, and holiday festivals, from about 1880 to the present.

NEW ARAB IMMIGRANT GROUPS

The two most important changes brought about by the U.S. Immigration Act of 1965 were the removal of regional immigration bans, and the removal of quotas that varied by country. No longer would persons from certain countries be favored over others, and there were no countries from which immigrants would not be accepted. After the law went into effect, the racial, ethnic, and religious makeup of the U.S. population changed significantly, as did the number of immigrants coming to the United States.

Arab immigrants arriving after 1965 were largely from the same countries as the Arab immigrants who came during the Great Migration of earlier years, with a few exceptions, such as the very large number of Egyptian immigrants; very few Egyptians came in previous decades. Another exception was Jordanians. The numbers for Jordanians are deceptive because about 80 percent of Jordanian immigrants were actually Palestinian. Palestinians have not been counted as Palestinians by the U.S. government, since the majority of the Palestinians are refugees and carry no passports, or carry passports from other countries.

A large Arab-American family from Yemen poses in their home in New York State in the 1970s. Yemenis were the sixth-largest group of immigrants to come to the United States after 1965.

The majority of the post-1965 Arab immigrants were families, unlike earlier Arabs who came on their own seeking wealth and opportunities. Some were very highly educated and worked as professionals, but many others were less educated. Some came to the United States primarily for an education, either for themselves or their children. Almost all were looking for a better economic life. The new Arab immigrants built on the foundations of the earlier arrivals and expanded the size, diversity, and geographic locations of their communities. In general, Arab immigrants were found in three major occupational groups: highly educated professionals, such as doctors and engineers; independent businesspersons, particularly shopkeepers; and factory workers, especially in auto-related industries. The most significant change in the overall picture of Arab immigrants who came to the United States after 1965 is that a much larger percentage, perhaps 60 percent, were Muslim. In earlier days more than 80 percent were Christian. Although

Muslims were part of the early Arab migration, few of them chose to bring their families over.

Lebanon sent more Arab immigrants to the United States after 1965 than any other Arab country, second only to the Palestinians, whose country of origin was not recognized as such. The numbers of Lebanese rose dramatically in 1976 and hit a peak in 1977. Lebanese immigration was heavily composed of newly immigrating families, many of them Muslims. Two major events occurred that help explain the peaks. In 1975 a civil war began in Lebanon, and many Lebanese refugees opted to come to the United States because they had relatives already there. Others were immigrants starting a new family migration.

After the Palestinians and Lebanese, Egyptians were the third-largest group of Arab immigrants to come to the United States after 1965. Unlike other large Arab immigrant groups, Egyptians did not begin to immigrate in significant numbers until the 1950s. The number of Egyptian immigrants in the United States began to increase significantly in 1967 and skyrocketed in 1970, when Gamal Abdel Nasser, the popular president of Egypt, died, and many Egyptians who thought they could find a better life elsewhere left their homeland. Egyptian immigrants tended to be highly educated professionals, including doctors, dentists, lawyers, scientists, and professors. Most of them brought their families. A large number were Coptic Christian, some were Protestant, and many others were Muslim. Unlike other Arab immigrants, a high percentage of Egyptians entered the United States as professionals whose services were needed in the United States. Iraqis, including Arabs, Chaldeans, and Assyrians, were the fourth-largest group of immigrants from the Arab world to the United States, and were highly educated. The Syrians were the fifth-largest group of Arab immigrants to come to the United States after 1965, followed by Yemenis as the sixth-largest group.

As these Arab immigrants learned to speak English and adjusted to life in the United States, they assisted friends and relatives who also wished to immigrate. After many years, some of the immigrants who initially planned to return to their home country decided instead to stay and began to bring their families over. As Arab immigrants settled, they established their own communities.

PROFESSIONS AND OCCUPATIONS

Among the third wave of Arab Americans, over 60 percent worked as executives, professionals, salespeople, administrative support personnel, and service personnel. Arab Americans were involved in every type of occupation imaginable. Arab-American parents often encouraged their children to enter into professional careers and become doctors, lawyers, engineers, and pharmacists. Others became teachers, professors, nurses, athletes, musicians, police officers, firefighters, and politicians. Many were employed in industry. Arab immigrants remained connected to automotive manufacturing in the Detroit area, where Arab communities surrounded automotive plants.

Three Responses to Immigration

Arab immigrants arriving after 1965 responded to their move to the United States in three main ways: (1) resisting assimilation with the attitude that migration was temporary, (2) fully integrating Arab cultures and customs into their new life in the United States, and (3) creating a division between public and private life, with the home and family structured in a manner similar to that in the Middle East. Arab Americans adapted to life in the United States by integrating Arab cultures and customs with the prevailing U.S. norms and trends. As the home was frequently considered a refuge for family and heritage, some Arab Americans drew a line between the public and private, between American and Arab. In this scenario, outside the house, Arab-American men and women interacted easily and extensively with coworkers, clients, or customers who were not predominantly Arab. At home, the relations between family members as well as the food and décor reflected influences from the Middle East.

In this context, Arab-American parents faced a choice of approaches when raising their children. Overall, they tended to teach their children how to behave by example and discipline, especially in response to dangerous situations. The interconnectedness of more unassimilated communities ran counter to the widespread U.S. social system that valued individualism, independence, and egalitarian relationships. For second- and third-generation Arab Americans, the family interconnectedness and hierarchy was sometimes suffocating. When faced with the rebellion of their children, Arab-American parents had a choice: either adapt to the mainstream American culture, giving their children more freedom by loosening the traditional Arab family structure; or discipline their children more within the family context.

Interconnectivity and a strong sense of family were passed down from generation to generation, regardless of the family's length of time in the United States. Arab family members also showed solidarity and familial loyalty by taking care of elderly parents. In the Arab world, age is respected, and elderly parents live with their children, usually with the eldest son and his family.

An Arab-American father and son outside a mosque in New York in the mid-1970s.

When these new immigrants arrived in an already-established Arab community with more family networks, and sometimes more education and financial resources, they were often able to establish themselves more quickly than earlier immigrants. Even with these advantages, however, many newer immigrants faced the same challenges as earlier arrivals. Some had difficulties finding jobs in the same fields in which they were employed back in their home countries. Another barrier was that many immigrants came from war-torn countries such as Lebanon and Palestine, an experience that made adjustment to their new life more difficult.

While recent immigrants followed the same general path as earlier arrivals, they did so at a faster pace. For instance, new immigrants did not have to go through the process of building their financial reserves through such traditional occupations as peddling. By using family resources accumulated through years of living in the United States, some new immigrants were able to quickly establish themselves and get a business running in a relatively short time. Another reason for quicker success was that earlier immigrants already paved the way for them to be successful.

The history of Arab-American work has been long and varied in the United States. Despite the different trends and evolutionary steps, there were common themes that characterized how Arab Americans continued to contribute to the American social and economic system in the 1970s. One was the spirit of entrepreneurship, which has come to define the Arab experience and is still strong today. Arab Americans established professional businesses, law offices, and computer sales and service businesses. Family was another factor for success. When asked about the secret behind Arab-American success, the most common answer people gave was family support and the ability of families to work together. Arab-American economic success was also due to the importance of education. Arab Americans had higher levels of high school and college education than the general U.S. population and many other ethnic groups.

A SHIFT IN ASSIMILATION AND ACCEPTANCE

Sometimes cultural and religious differences affected how Arab Americans were treated in public schools. The girls often wore the *hijab*, a headscarf that covers the hair and neck, which made them stand out from other students. In schools where there were both Christian and Muslim students, there were differences in how holidays were celebrated. Because of religious and cultural reasons, some Arab-American Muslim girls did not participate in after-school activities and sports, or in physical education and music classes. Foreign-born Arab-American students also had difficulties adapting to the American public school systems because they were brought up in a society with different values. Some Arab-American parents felt uncomfortable with the more relaxed discipline system in American public schools, and some even chose

Arab-American schoolgirls, some wearing the hijab and some without it, in Lackawanna, New York, around 1977. Muslim Arab girls sometimes had more difficulty than boys in adapting to American public schools because of their attire and other religious values.

to send their children to private or religious schools. Private Islamic schools were offered as an alternative to the public school system. In general, Islamic schools in the United States were places in which the more established Muslim Arab-American families could preserve cultural and religious roots, and where newly arrived immigrants could find a community with which they could communicate during their adjustment to American life.

Although many earlier Arab immigrants felt pressure to assimilate into American society, with the new flow of immigrants to the United States, many changes occurred in Arab-American families. By the turn of the 21st century there was less pressure to assimilate or forget Arab culture. This was partially due to the fact that cultural diversity became a more accepted part of American society. The large numbers of recent immigrants also increased the sense of connection with the Arab world among Arab Americans. Many Arab Americans were more willing to display, rather than ignore, their Arab customs and values. In general, children were not pressured to assimilate, but rather to preserve their Arab culture. Most Arab Americans attached great importance to the family. They often explained that the family allowed them to preserve many of the customs that they held dear, and to maintain their religion and language.

DISCRIMINATION MEETS POLITICAL ACTION

Arab Americans became a vital part of American society, yet they often faced discriminatory or unfair treatment on the basis of their group identity. Arab Americans organized to oppose discrimination and educate the public about Arab Americans and the Arab cultural heritage. They had yet to fully convey to their fellow Americans, however, the true picture of their historical, social, and cultural identity. Arab Americans also continued to suffer violations of their civil rights, leading to the establishment of such organizations as the American-Arab Anti-Discrimination Committee (ADC), which was founded to protect the rights of Arab Americans. After the late 1970s there was an

Even though Iranians are not Arabs, during the 1979 Iran Hostage Crisis, Americans sometimes aimed their anger at Middle Eastern Americans in general. This group carried signs with racist and xenophobic messages during a protest in Washington, D.C., in November 1979.

increase in hate crimes—personal attacks based on ethnic prejudice—against Arab Americans.

The 1970s was a period when many Arab Americans became convinced that the more controversial Middle East politics became, and the greater the misunderstandings about Arab causes, the more important it was to be active in public affairs. The political activism of the 1970s brought negative attention to Arab-American groups. As the Israeli-Palestinian conflict continued and Palestinian resistance to Israeli policies increased, Arab Americans and their allies were often viewed suspiciously, or as "anti-American," by U.S. government agencies. This attitude became worse during the late 1970s. Higher oil prices leading to U.S. gasoline shortages fostered a climate in which Arabs were commonly perceived as enemies to the country. Arab stereotypes with political and economic roots infiltrated American popular culture, which portrayed Arab characters as villains. The American public began to think of Arabs as enemies. Arab Americans saw the need to work hard to correct these images and protect themselves from public backlash. Even when problems happened in non-Arab countries, such as the 1979 U.S. hostage crisis in Iran, the backlash resulted in negative feelings about Middle Eastern people as a whole.

THE PULL OF INDIVIDUAL FREEDOM

The right of individuals to take pride in and display their ethnicity was a pull factor for immigrants from all over the world. Other pull factors were the political institutions, tolerance of differences, and the guarantees of individual rights in the United States. Most of the post-1965 immigrants were Muslims who valued the freedom to worship and the ability to establish mosques. The right to worship was also important to many Christians who immigrated after 1965. The rise of multiculturalism during the 1970s increased tolerance for differences and allowed for expression of heritage, language, and customs.

Freedom of expression was a welcome change from the anti-immigrant climate of the early 20th century, when Arab Americans lost many of their distinctly ethnic traits and traditions in public in the process of assimilation. However, as a result of the civil rights movement, Arab Americans experienced an ethnic revival. Many of the new arrivals, and second and third generations alike, adopted the broad label of Arab American and formed political and social organizations. Networks helped the newcomers with places to stay, loans, and assistance in renting apartments, finding jobs, and enrolling in schools or universities. Arab-American small business owners sometimes hired family members and friends, making it easier for immigrants to find their first jobs in the United States, particularly if they were unskilled and knew little English. Some Arab American–owned businesses catering to a predominantly Arab-American clientele concentrated in areas with Arabic grocery stores, bakeries, restaurants, and Arabic-language bookshops and

Middle Eastern students marching during the Iran Hostage Crisis in Lafayette Park in Washington, D.C., in August 1980; such demonstrations were met with hecklers and counter-demonstrations. The crisis received intense media coverage in the United States and lasted until 1981.

video stores. Some communities were able to establish networks from an ethnic safety net, allowing for the cohesion, safety, security, and prosperity of Arab families through interaction, assistance, and intervention.

ARAB AMERICANS IN THE MEDIA

After the 1970s, the image of Arabs presented by Hollywood and the media worsened. Two main, gendered stereotypes prevailed—Arab men as terrorists and Arab women as submissive, veiled, shapeless beings. The prevalence of these images may have contributed to some of the discrimination and harassment Arab Americans suffered. However, Arab Americans continued to have a positive relationship with, and impact on, U.S. society through interfaith councils, parent-teacher associations, school boards, rotary clubs, and chambers of commerce on the local level, but were less active in political advocacy. To maintain their identity and preserve their culture, Arab Americans began to organize gatherings centered around music, dance, literature, and art. The mahrajans, or festivals, that had been popular among Arab Americans between the 1930s and 1960s witnessed a revival in many Arab-American communities around the country. In all of these festivals, music was the most important component that brought the community together. Local Arab-American musicians, singers, and dance groups performed to large audiences.

CONCLUSION

In sum, the third-wave Arab immigrants carried a greater burden of interne-cine conflict than did previous waves, and hence were less likely than previous groups to consider returning home. At the same time, because so many of the third-wave immigrants were highly educated, they felt a greater drive to par-ticipate in political groups that grew in the wake of the 1967 and 1973 Arab-Israeli wars. With the homeland still fresh in their minds, this group of immi-grants was ready to get involved in the frustrating task of lobbying in order to have an effect on U.S. policymakers, unlike earlier immigrants, who tended to be isolated. More angry with America with regards to its policies, the third wave immigrants paradoxically made more enthusiastic Americans.

KHODR M. ZAAROUR
SHAW UNIVERSITY AND NORTH CAROLINA CENTRAL UNIVERSITY

Further Reading

Ameri, Anan and Dawn Ramey. *Arab American Encyclopedia*. Detroit, MI: Library of Congress, 2000.

Boosahad, Elizabeth. *Arab-American Faces and Voices: The Origins of an Immigrant Community*. Austin, TX: University of Texas Press, 2003.

Hooglund, Eric J. *Crossing the Waters*. Washington, D.C.: Smithsonian Insti-tution Press, 1987.

Kayyali, Randa A. *The Arab Americans: The New Americans*. Westport, CT: Greenwood Press, 2006.

Naff, Alixa. *Becoming American: The Early Arab Immigrant Experience*. Car-bondale, IL: Southern Illinois University Press, 1985.

Orfalea, Gregory. *Before the Flames: A Quest for the History of Arab Ameri-cans*. Austin, TX: University of Texas Press, 1988.

———. *The Arab Americans*. Northampton, MA: Interlink Publishing, 2006.

Schur, Joan Broadsky. *The Arabs: Coming to America*. Detroit, MI: Thom-son/Gale, 2005.

Younis, Adele L. *The Coming of the Arabic-Speaking People to the United States*. New York: Library of Congress, 1995.

CHAPTER 8

The Eighties: 1980 to 1989

ACCORDING TO 1990 U.S. Census figures, 870,000 people identified themselves as Arab or from an Arab country. However, studies have shown that Arab Americans were significantly undercounted, and the true number by the end of the 1980s was somewhere between one and two million. Some reluctance to officially identify as a member of a minority group and suspicion of government authorities may help account for the difference between counted and actual figures. By the 1980s the large majority of Arab Americans were native-born U.S. citizens.

Everyday life for many Arab Americans in the 1980s centered around family, work, cultural expression, customs, traditions, and beliefs. Similar to other ethnic minorities in the United States that have tried to preserve their cultures, Arab Americans placed emphasis on sharing culture daily at home, as well as on special occasions at large community gatherings. Passing their culture down from generation to generation in this manner was not always easy, however, as they had to balance between adapting to a new culture, and retaining older traditional values and ways.

RELIGIOUS BELIEFS AND PRACTICES

Although most Arabs worldwide were Muslim, most Arab Americans were Christians in the 1980s. The majority of these Christians belonged to different

Islam in Brief

About 1,400 years ago in the Arabian city of Mecca (now Saudi Arabia) the Prophet Muhammad began preaching the message of Islam, which was that there was only one God (Allah, in Arabic). Muslims are believers in Islam, which means "submission" (submission to the will of Allah). They believe that Muhammad was the last in a series of prophets, Jesus having been one of them, through whom Allah revealed the best way for people to live. The holy book for Muslims is the Koran (Qur'an) and is believed to contain the words of Allah as revealed to Muhammad in 622 c.e. Friday is the day of group worship for Muslims, and their house of group worship is called a mosque (or *masjid*, which means "a place for prostration").

There are two major offshoots of Muslims: the Sunni and Shi'ites (Shia). The Sunni make up about 80 percent of Muslims in the world and are the majority of Arab-American Muslims. The two sects agree about the teachings of Islam, but disagree as to who should have been the rightful leader (caliph) of the Muslims after Muhammad's death in 632 c.e.

There are five pillars of Islam to which every Muslim is required to adhere: 1) *Shahada* is the believer's profession that there is no God but Allah, and that Muhammad is the messenger of Allah. 2) *Salat* is prayer five times per day: at dawn, noon, mid-afternoon, sunset, and dusk. 3) *Zakat* relates to social responsibility, and requires the believer to give a portion of his or her wealth back to the community or to those in need. 4) *Saum* refers to the observance of Ramadan, which requires fasting during that month. 5) *Hajj*, the pilgrimage to Mecca, the city in Saudi Arabia where Muslims believe Muhammad first received revelations from Allah, is a journey believers try to accomplish at least once. There, all pilgrims are dressed alike and seen as equal as they assemble around a single center, the *Ka'aba*.

The Masjid Al-Faatir (which means mosque of the originator, or Allah) in the Kenwood area of Chicago was founded in 1984 with financial assistance from the boxer Muhammad Ali and his manager Jabir Muhammad.

denominations of the Christian Orthodox Church, such as the Antiochian, Coptic, Syrian, and Greek Orthodox churches. Other Arab-American Christians belonged to the Uniate churches: formerly Orthodox groups that had affiliated with the Roman Catholic Church. These included Chaldean, Maronite, and Greek Catholic denominations. Arab-American Sunni and Shi'ite (Shia) Muslims—two distinct sects—and those of the Druze faith were also in America in significant numbers. The Druze are a religious community found primarily in Lebanon, Syria, and Israel whose traditional religion is said to have begun as an offshoot of Islam. Another offshoot of Islam is Sufism, considered a mystical branch where believers seek truth and inner spiritual growth by seeking communion with Allah through love and devotion. Although a small minority among Muslims, they have throughout the ages been very influential in spreading the word of Islam, serving as role models for pious living.

Christian Arab Americans were not encumbered by the same kinds of restraints as Muslims when attempting to practice their religious beliefs. For example, Muslims are required to pray ritualistically five times a day, and to join in communal prayer, *jumaa*, on Fridays. In the 1980s they had difficulty within places of employment and schools in adhering to these practices, and sometimes had to resign themselves to not participating.

RELIGIOUS HOLIDAYS
Throughout the 1980s Arab Americans continued to celebrate many religious and cultural holidays. Christian Arab Americans celebrated Christmas like many Americans. Even some non-Christian Arab Americans sometimes put up Christmas trees and shared gifts. Arab Americans also enjoyed other American holidays, such as Thanksgiving and the Fourth of July, during which times they ate both traditional Arab foods and American foods. Other holy days, such as Ramadan, Eid al-Fitr, and Eid al-Adha, were celebrated only by Muslims.

Eid al-Fitr is the feast Muslims have at the end of Ramadan, the holy month each year (occurring at different times according to their lunar calendar), when they fast from sunup to sundown each day of the month. Not even one drop of water may pass their mouths during fasting. Smoking and sexual relations are also not indulged in at the times of fasting during Ramadan, which is a time of sacrifice and cleansing. Another significant holiday for Muslims is Eid al-Adha, when the remembrance of the sacrifice of Ibrahim as told in the Qur'an (Abraham, as told in the Bible) is celebrated. Ibrahim proved his obedience to Allah by his willingness to sacrifice his son Ishmael. An angel substituted a lamb instead, so Ishmael was spared. Muslims sacrifice and slaughter animals for food (usually sheep) during this time, and have feasts. During Eid al-Adha, scores of Muslims travel to Mecca in Saudi Arabia for the Muslim pilgrimage of hajj, to renew their dedication to Allah and receive the new title of *Hajj* or

Animals such as this cow are sometimes decorated in colorful beads during the Muslim holiday of Eid al-Adha. Some urban Muslims who are unable to slaughter their own animals in the United States and other countries visit a slaughterhouse or farm for the sacrifice.

Hajja for men and women, respectively. The holy days of Ramadan, Eid al-Fitr, and Eid al-Adha were not recognized by most Americans in the 1980s, and did not excuse students from classes or workers from their jobs. However, as the population of Muslims increased, notations of these globally celebrated holidays were increasingly included on American calendars.

CLOTHING AND FOOD

In the 1980s Arab Americans generally did not wear traditional Arab clothing in public. Occasionally, some recently immigrated women and a few Arab-American and Muslim women would wear a long, traditional dress, a *kaftan* or *jalaba*. More commonly seen were new immigrant women and some native-born, Arab-American women wearing a headscarf called a hijab or *chador*. They were worn in a manner common to each woman's place of family origin. Very few women wore *niqab*, which covered the entire face except for the eyes, unless these women were extremely strict about their adherence to Islam. Men usually wore mainstream European and American clothing.

Food and sharing were main components in most events and gatherings among Arab Americans. Women usually prepared meals, although Arab male chefs were also common, and they worked to produce traditional dishes that were reminiscent of the homeland. The cuisine was usually a cultural diffusion from their country of origin, although climate and location were additional factors. The food was reflective of items easily obtained in their native geographical area. For example, the foods of desert nomads and caravans that could be transported easily, such as sheep, goats, camels, rice, dates, and other dried fruits were common.

Arab-American cuisine had similarities no matter where each family originated. They relied heavily upon items not readily found in every American kitchen, which gave the dishes a distinctive taste: dates, figs, olives, olive oil, sesame seeds, chick peas, lentils, fava beans, and feta cheese. Herbs and seasonings common to the Arab-American diet were cumin, coriander, saffron, sugar, mint, cinnamon, nutmeg, and mustard. Many vegetables like eggplant, zucchini, green peppers, tomatoes, cabbage, and grape leaves were made into labor-intensive, traditional dishes.

Lamb was also a common dish. For Arab-American Muslims, pork was prohibited by their religion, but Arab-American Christians also refrained from eating pork for cultural reasons. Muslims were required to consume meat that was ritually slaughtered, called halal (according to Islamic law and therefore allowable). Fish and chicken were less frequently part of the cuisine.

This Ramadan feast includes bread, dates, vegetables, and salads similar to those frequently encountered in Arab-American households.

Breads and teas, especially mint tea, and rich coffee were consumed on a regular basis. Rice and couscous (made from semolina) were staples to many Arab-American diets. Pistachio nuts, almonds, and walnuts were welcome treats. Traditionally prepared pastries, as well as fruits like grapes, oranges, melons and pomegranates, were to be found at any Arab-American table. Usually whatever the meal, the bread was warm, the salads fresh, the main course richly seasoned, and fruit or nuts plus a pastry dish was nearby. A single man who came from one Arab country to America once commented, "I never had cold bread until I came to the United States." This small adjustment spoke to the kind of attention given to Arab-American food preparation, serving, and eating, which is intrinsic to the Arab culture.

Arab Americans usually purchase food regularly so that it will be fresh, rather than food from cans and packages. In Arab countries of origin, the largest meal was typically eaten at midday, with all of the family members present at the table, young and old alike. But in 1980s America, with family members usually at work or school during the day, this custom began to change. Like most Americans, the family meal was usually consumed in the late evening. Meals were usually eaten in households, unless special events or parties were attended. Christian Arabs were allowed to drink alcoholic beverages on occasion, but conservative Muslims refrained from drinking alcohol.

DANCE

There is a wide array of dance in the Arab-American community, and the belly dancing that many Americans are aware of is not the rule for most Arab Americans. Belly dancing may have originated in Egypt, and is native to North Africa and Asia. In the Arabic language it is known as *raqs sharqi*, meaning "Oriental dance;" or *raqs baladi*, meaning "dance of country" or "folk dance." Some believe it was part of regional, traditional birthing practices. In those regions, native girls and boys learned it informally through observation and imitation at an early age. During gatherings with family and friends, belly dancing was usually performed wearing a *kaftan* (native dress that reaches the ankles) with a scarf or belt tied around the hips to accentuate the movements. Beaded bras and skimpy, revealing skirts are usually worn by dancers in nightclubs and for the entertainment of tourists.

There were other traditional dances performed at community and private gatherings that were specific to particular regions, like the *debka* (line dancing) of Palestinians at weddings, as well as *debkas* from other Arab countries. There were other dances reserved for religious life, like the whirling of the Dervishes, and the trance dancing of those who practiced Sufism. But for the most part, and especially for the younger generations, Arab Americans enjoyed the social dancing that most Americans enjoyed. Men and women danced together, unlike in many Arab homelands where dancing was often men with men who danced in an area separate from the women who danced together.

MUSIC AND ENTERTAINMENT

The records of Om Kulthum, Fairuz, Farid al-Atrash, his sister Asmahan, and other singers from the Arab world could be heard on record players in many Arab-American households during the 1980s. Om Kulthum (Mother Kulthum) was an Egyptian classical singer, songwriter, and actress, and although she died in 1975, her music remained popular throughout the 1980s. In fact, she was the Arab world's most famous and distinguished singer of the 20th century, affectionately called "the Star of the East" (*kawkub el-sharq*) by those who loved her music. She had great vocal capacity. Her music was noted for its long contralto ranged rifts (sometimes an hour's length), in Arabic, winding in, out, and around the background classical instrumentation (mostly violins and lutes). Her concerts, consisting of two or three songs, would typically last from three to six hours. Love, longing, and loss were usually the themes of her musical presentations.

Fairuz, a singer and musician from Lebanon, drew large audiences with her music through the 1980s and beyond. She masterfully blended her cultural motifs during performances with diverse music from Mozart, Latin America, and the Balkans. She also recorded Christian hymns as well as pro-Palestinian songs.

There were many other great Arab musical and film artists. Egypt has often led in the production of Arabic music and film. In addition to Arabic music and film, Arab Americans also found fame in American music, film, and television, as was evidenced by some Arab-American celebrities of that time period, such as radio personality Casey Kasem, film producer Moustapha Akkad, dancer and singer Paula Abdul, Oscar winner F. Murray Abraham, comedian and entertainer Danny Thomas, actor Jamie Farr, NFL player Doug Flutie, and Van Halen singer Sammy Hagar. Paula Abdul rose from being a cheerleader for the Los Angeles Lakers NBA basketball team to being a sought-after choreographer at the height of the music video era, then to becoming a Pop-R&B singer with a string of hits in the late 1980s and early 1990s. She sold over 53 million records and scored six number-one singles on the Billboard Hot 100, placing her in a tie for fifth among the female solo performers who have reached number one.

Singer, dancer, choreographer, and television star Paula Abdul, who got her start in the late 1980s, is of Syrian and French descent.

EDUCATION

The Prophet Muhammad was believed to have said, "It is the duty of every Muslim man and woman to seek education." Under his encouragement and influence, Arab Muslims pursued knowledge for its own sake. Education has traditionally been very important to Arabs, who traveled to cities near and far seeking knowledge from different masters. Books were collected from all over the world to create monumental libraries, housing volumes on medicine, philosophy, mathematics, science, alchemy, logic, astronomy, and a wide array of other subjects.

In the 1980s and beyond, education was still of great value to Arabs and Arab Americans. The wave of Arab immigrants to the United States after World War II, unlike the majority in the wave prior to it, was comprised of those who already had college degrees or those who would earn them.

GENDER ROLES

There were many cultural issues surrounding the adjustment to life in the United States that were controversial for most immigrants and their descendents. Arab Americans were no exception. One important issue was gender roles, or the different roles of men, women, boys, and girls in a family. For some Arab Americans, especially Muslims from rural areas, this meant dressing modestly and socializing less with children of the opposite sex beyond a certain age. Men were favored and indulged. They were encouraged to attend college and become entrepreneurs and professionals in many fields such as science, engineering, medicine, and law.

Much has been speculated about Arab and Arab-American women in relationship to Arab and Arab-American men. Women worked in the home to make it comfortable for the entire family. Some Arab-American women attended college or worked professionally, but for the most part, men were their passports to worlds beyond the home. However, involvement in social and philanthropic organizations became a calling for many of these women in the 1980s. As they worked hard at home, they also worked hard for their communities. Arab-American women had more freedom to shape their own lives in America than they would have had in their native homelands.

MARRIAGE AND FAMILY

Love was considered a desirable and natural part of life. Premarital sex was shunned. Dating was discouraged, especially for unchaperoned women, in consideration of conservative tradition. Dating did occur, and a balance was sought between old and new worlds. However, female chastity and honor was highly valued. A trial period of ritual engagement allowed for a type of dating among Arab-American Muslims. And in some instances, Arab-American parents still arranged the marriage of their son or daughter to someone they felt would be responsible and provide a good home for them and for their grandchildren. The family would seek a future son- or daughter-in-law from the same culture, background, and religious belief. There was a preference within Arab culture for endogamous (within the same community, tribe, or clan) marriages, especially between cousins. Although not uniform throughout the Arab society, and not strong among some Christian groups, it was a preference among Muslim groups. Second- and third-generation Arab Americans did frequently marry those who were not of their culture, background, and religion, but less so if they were Muslim. A woman who was not Muslim, but marrying

A Muslim woman with her daughter. The title of Om is a sign of respect for mothers in a number of Arab cultures.

Om and *Abu*

In some Arab countries, when an Arab woman became a mother for the first time, the title of *Om* or *Umm* (meaning mother or mother of) was placed before the name of her first child, and this became the mother's new name for life. Similarly, when an Arab man became a father for the first time, the title of *Abu* (meaning father or father of) was placed before the name of his first child, thus becoming the father's new, lifelong name. The name change reflected an upgrade in one's status in life. The parent was proud to carry such a title (just as Muslim men and women were proud to have the new title of Hajj or Hajja after they made their pilgrimage to Mecca). Children were so valued in the Arab culture that to have them was one important way of denoting the arrival of manhood or womanhood.

A young Muslim in Cambridge, Massachusetts, praying with her grandmother.

a Muslim man, would more than likely convert to Islam. A Muslim woman was encouraged to marry a Muslim man even if he was not an Arab, in consideration of family feelings and future children.

Many Arab-American families tended to be very close. Extended family members often resided in the same household with the nuclear family members, making it a household of three, and sometimes four generations. If extended family did not live with them, then they usually lived nearby, and were very involved in each other's lives. Arab Americans also tried to maintain contact with extended family that remained in their country and town of origin, as well as those who were dispersed around the world. Sometimes this involved Arab men who came to America for opportunity and prosperity, while leaving their wives and children in another part of the world, returning for visits whenever they were able. For the families who lived together in America, children were most often treated adoringly and with patience, although in a strict manner in order to shelter them from the perceived evils of American society.

Arab-American families might have included immigrants from several decades, as well as American-born citizens of different generational groups. Although different perceptions about life and the world were evident between the younger and older generations, respect for elders without question was a hallmark in the relationships between the generations. More Americanized and younger Arab Americans sometimes saw the older generations of women as interfering too much in the lives of the younger family members, and the older men as being slow at making decisions and arguing about petty issues. The older generations of Arab-American men and women were affected by their recollections of the sacrifices they made to pave their way in America.

Despite gains of wealth and other amenities, such as freedom from political persecutions, some older generations of Arab Americans wondered if such gains were worth losing their offspring to the American trappings that took them further away from their beliefs and traditions.

ADVOCACY AND MEDIA

Advocacy organizations rose to prominence in the 1980s, as a growing number of public figures began to identify themselves as Arab American. Some important posts were held by Arab Americans, including White House Chief of Staff John H. Sununu (1989–91) and U.S. Senate Majority Leader George Mitchell (1980–95). Arab Americans became increasingly visible in the fields of entertainment, science, sports, and industry.

Yet there were other reasons for the rise to prominence of advocacy organizations in the 1980s, among them relentless stereotyping and even racial profiling of Arabs and Arab Americans. Such perceptions heaped harassment, hate crimes, and violence upon many Arab Americans. Arab-American publications addressed these and other issues of concern for the Arab American.

Activism through press and media increased in the Arab-American community in the 1980s. Founded in 1981, *The Arabic Hour* was a nonprofit, weekly television program produced by the American-Arab Broadcasting Network, Inc., presenting culture, news, music, cuisine, and interviews concerning the events and issues of the Arab world and the Arab-American experience. The program aired in English and included entertainment in Arabic. The show was made possible through the contributions of professional volunteers who wished to preserve Arab-American heritage and culture. The *American Arab Scientific Society Newsletter* was founded in New York City in 1983 as a quarterly newsletter covering the activities of the scientific society. The Arab-American Press Guild (AAPG) began on January 17, 1985, in Los Angeles, California, to serve Arab-American journalists and to coordinate the media of the community and the Arab-American world in the United States. Another monthly newsletter was founded in 1987 in Davis, California, providing a nonpartisan and nonprofit forum for constructive ideas primarily concerning the Middle East. It was published in English.

POLITICS AND ARAB-AMERICAN LIFE IN THE 1980s

"The 1980s were a difficult time for Arab Americans. Politicians returned our contributions, rejected our endorsements, and many effectively hung 'No Arab Americans allowed' signs on their campaign doors. Back then, we called it 'the politics of exclusion.' We fought back. We organized, worked hard, and we emerged victorious—or, should I say, somewhat victorious?" These are the words of Dr. James Zogby, a longtime Arab-American political activist. In 1982 he cofounded Save Lebanon, Inc., a private, humanitarian, nonprofit,

The Murder of Alex Odeh

During much of the 1980s, Arab Americans lived in an ever-increasing state of anxiety as all Americans witnessed President Ronald Reagan's administration wage war on international terrorism. Tensions were heightened when two U.S. attacks against Libya and U.S. involvement in Lebanon after Israel's invasion of Lebanon occurred in 1982. When an American passenger airplane was hijacked in Europe en route to Lebanon, it triggered a backlash against Arab Americans, Middle Easterners, and Muslims in the United States. Another hijacking occurred in 1985.

Alex Odeh was born into a Palestinian Christian family in Jifna, Palestine in 1944 and immigrated to the United States in 1972. He became the Director of the Los Angeles office of the American Arab Anti-Discrimination Committee (ADC). On October 10, 1985, the 41-year-old Odeh appeared on local television, expressing his opinion that the Palestine Liberation Organization (PLO) and Yasir Arafat, its leader, were not responsible for the October 7 hijacking of the *Achille Lauro* cruise liner in the Mediterranean by Palestinian terrorists. The following day a bomb went off in ADC's Los Angeles office, killing Odeh. After an FBI investigation, it was suspected that members of the Jewish Defense League (JDL) were behind the bombing attack.

The Anti-Defamation League and the American Jewish Committee both condemned the murder. Irv Rubin, who that same year had become chairman of the JDL—a violent, extremist Jewish organization—immediately made several public statements in reaction to the incident. "I have no tears for Mr. Odeh," Rubin said. "He got exactly what he deserved." In 1994 when a memorial statue of Odeh was erected in Santa Ana, California, the JDL protested. In 1997 the statue was defaced. Nearly 25 years after Odeh's murder, no one had been charged in his death. Officials had not released the names of suspects, but Odeh's brother, Sami, claimed they were all disciples of the late Rabbi Meir Kahane, the anti-Arab founder of the JDL.

and nonsectarian relief organization that funded healthcare for Palestinian and Lebanese victims of war. Holding a doctorate in religion, he appeared on and hosted radio and television programs in the United States and abroad, wrote a weekly column for major newspapers, testified before the U.S. House and Senate Committees, and authored a number of books and articles about the plight of Arab Americans.

In the 1980s Arab Americans began to push back against ever-increasing stereotypes of Arabs and threats to Arabs in the United States. Arab immigrants who arrived in the 1970s and 1980s did not encounter a warm reception from the host society. Instead of assimilating, these new immigrants often opted to remain on the outskirts of the larger society, making their own in-group social connections in ethnic neighborhoods, while adopting many American cultural mores. This wave of immigrants was the driving force behind the upsurge in the establishment of Muslim schools, mosques, charities, and Arabic language classes. In 1980, shortly after a firebomb attack on the offices of the Palestine Human Rights Campaign (PHRC), a group of Arab Americans led by Dr. Zogby and former Senator James Abourezk of South Dakota founded the American Arab Anti-Discrimination Committee (ADC). The ADC began publishing its *ADC Times* in 1980 as a monthly membership newsletter in Connecticut and Washington, D.C. The organization had some success in sensitizing the news media to issues of stereotyping, although stereotyping continued in other domains like the entertainment media, especially in movies and television.

Dr. Zogby founded another organization in the 1980s called the Arab American Institute (AAI), which was established in 1985 and based in Washington, D.C. Dr. Zogby served as its president. A nonprofit, nonpartisan, national leadership organization, AAI was created to nurture and encourage the direct participation of Arab Americans in political and civic life in the United States. Such foundations were not laid easily, and Dr. Zogby described hardships such as accusations of terrorism, exclusion from political coalitions, threats, harassment of universities and media outlets that invited him to speak, isolation, and even threats on his life. In 1985, during attacks on ADC offices in a number of cities, ADC West Coast Director Alex Odeh was murdered. His unsolved murder was considered the top terrorist act of 1985 and it continues to be highly significant for Arab Americans.

CONCLUSION

By the mid-1980s, the perception that many Arabs had terrorist ties was prevalent in American society. An example of this attitude swirled around the streets of Dearborn, Michigan, where a fifth of the population was Arabic-speaking and the muezzin boomed out the call to prayer five times a day. Although the town was enriched by Arab coffee houses, shops, and restaurants, the mayor, Michael Guido, helped to ensure his election by promising to deal with the Arab "problem." In fact, Arab Americans in Michigan were in "a zone of danger," according to FBI Director William Webster, and were afraid that American frustration over Middle Eastern terrorism would erupt into local violence.

In 1987 numerous Immigration and Naturalization Service (INS), FBI, and police agents raided several houses in Los Angeles, arresting six Palestinians and the Kenyan wife of one of the men. Days later, another Palestinian man was arrested while sitting to take a community college exam. The arrested persons became known as the L.A. Eight. They reportedly were caught up in a three-year investigation into the activities of Arab-American activists, and were scheduled for deportation. Many who rallied to their defense feared they would be set up as an example to anyone who dared to question U.S. foreign policy in the Middle East. Subsequently it was reported that a copy of a secret INS plan had been obtained that outlined how the U.S. government planned to apprehend, detain, and deport large numbers of Arab and Iranian students, permanent residents, and American citizens in the event the president declared a state of emergency. The necessity for effective Arab-American responses to discrimination and suspicion would only grow in the decade to follow, as the United States reeled from a number of smaller terrorist incidents leading up to the attacks of September 11, 2001.

DENISE HINDS-ZAAMI
PENNSYLVANIA STATE UNIVERSITY

Further Reading

Abraham, Sameer Y., ed., and Nabeel Abraham. *The Arab World and Arab-Americans: Understanding a Neglected Minority.* Detroit, MI: Wayne State University. Center for Urban Studies, 1981.

———. *Arabs in the New World. Studies on Arab-American Communities.* Detroit, MI: Wayne State University. Center for Urban Studies, 1983.

Arab American National Museum. Available online, URL: www.Arab AmericanMuseum.org. Accessed December 18, 2008.

De la Cruz, Patricia G., and Angela Brittingham. "The Arab Population: 2000." *United States Census 2000.* Available online, URL: www .census.gov. Accessed December 18, 2008.

Feagin, Joe R. *Racist America: Roots, Current Realities and Future Reparations.* Lanham, MD: Routledge, 2000.

"The Great History of the Arab People and Civilization." *Introduction to the Arab World.* Available online, URL: www.middleeastnews.com/ introarab101.html. Accessed September 16, 2008.

Haiek, Joseph R. *Arab-American Almanac.* 4th ed. Glendale, CA: News Circle, 1992.

Jamal, Amaney, ed., and Nadine Naber. *Race and Arab Americans Before and After 9/11. From Invisible Citizens to Visible Subjects.* Syracuse, NY: Syracuse University, 2008.

Marvasti, Amir, and Karyn D. McKinney. *Middle Eastern Lives in America.* Lanham, MD: Rowman & Littlefield, 2004.

Samhan, Helen Hatab. "By the Numbers." *Arab American Market.* Allied Media Corp. Available online, URL: www.allied-media.com. Accessed November 21, 2008.

Shakir, Evelyn. *Bint Arab. Arab and Arab American Women in the United States.* Westport, CT: Praeger, 1997.

Suleiman, Michael, ed. *Arabs in America: Building a New Future.* Philadelphia, PA: Temple University, 1999.

Zogby, James. "Are Arab Americans People Like Us?" Arab American Institute. Available online, URL: www.aaiusa.org. Accessed December 1, 2000.

———. *Al-Ahram Weekly/Cairo.* "Alarm Bells in America As Arab-Americans Face Increased Demonization." May 24, 2000. Available online, URL: www.commondreams.org. Accessed March 27, 2009.

CHAPTER 9

The Nineties: 1990 to 1999

ESTIMATES OF ARAB Americans living in the United States in the 1990s are at about three million. The 2000 U.S. Census accounted for some 1.25 million people who self-identified with an Arabic-speaking origin. Other indicators suggest approximately 3.5 million. It is difficult to obtain a more exact figure because the U.S. Census Bureau did not use the Arab-American classification as a distinct ethnicity. Also, people identified themselves in various ways. Some Arab Americans identified themselves as Middle Eastern, for example, or just Arab, as no single term encompassed all Americans of Arab ancestry. Others identified themselves according to their specific country of origin. In addition, recent immigrants from many countries are reluctant to give personal and confidential information to the government, and an increasing number of people have more than one ancestry group to which they belong. Choosing only one group, or choosing "other" on a form, can be misleading.

The U.S. Census Bureau considered as Arab all people with ancestries originating from Arabic-speaking countries or areas of the world categorized as Arab. For example, people who reported they were Arab, Egyptian, Iraqi, Jordanian, Lebanese, Middle Eastern, Moroccan, North African, Palestinian, Syrian, and so forth, were included in this category. Kurds and Berbers, who are not considered Arab by Arabs themselves, were also included as Arabs if they came from these places. Yet some groups from areas where people

The Islamic Cultural Center on Manhattan's Upper East Side was completed in 1991. The mosque was built at a 29-degree angle to Manhattan's grid of streets so that it faced Mecca.

consider themselves Arabs were not included, such as Mauritania, Somalia, Djibouti, the Sudan, and the Comoros Islands.

About 70,000 people of Arab ancestry lived in New York City by the end of the 1990s, making it the city with the largest Arab population in the United States. The next-highest Arab-populated cities were Los Angeles, Chicago, Houston, Philadelphia, Phoenix, San Diego, Dallas, San Antonio, and Detroit. Dearborn, Michigan, had the highest percentage of Arabs in its population, with 30 percent having Arab ancestry. Other cities with large proportions of Arabs were Sterling Heights, Warren, and Livonia in Michigan; Burbank, Glendale, and Daly in California; and Jersey City and Paterson in New Jersey.

Lebanese, Syrian, and Egyptian were the three Arab groups with the highest populations in the United States by the end of the 1990s. Percentages for the largest groups were Lebanese (34 percent), Syrian (11 percent), and Egyptian (11 percent), followed by Palestinians (6 percent), Jordanians (3 percent), Moroccans (3 percent), and Iraqis (3 percent). About 46 percent of Arab Americans were native U.S. citizens, while 54 percent were born outside of the United States. Arabs had a higher rate of naturalization to the United States (54 percent) than the overall foreign-born population (40 percent). For the decade after 1990, the Immigration and Naturalization Service (INS) estimated that more than 300,000 Arabs immigrated to America. According to research by the American Arab Anti-Discrimination Committee (ADC), nearly 63 percent of Arab Americans are Christian (35 percent Roman Catholic, 10 percent Protestant, and 18 percent Eastern Orthodox), with Muslims at just under 25 percent, although their numbers are on the rise.

PROMINENT ARAB AMERICANS IN THE 1990s

There were quite a few distinguished Arab Americans in the 1990s. Dr. Elias Corey (1928–), from Harvard University, won the 1990 Nobel Prize for chemistry, "for his development of the theory and methodology of organic synthesis." Dr. Michael DeBakey (1908–2008), whose parents were Lebanese immigrants, served as the Chancellor of Baylor University's College of Medicine. He pioneered the development of artificial hearts and heart pumps, and continued his innovative work throughout the 1990s. Arab-American lunar geologist Dr. Farouk El-Baz continued his work with NASA that began in the late 1960s when he assisted in the planning of the Apollo moon landings.

Noted scholar Edward W. Said (1935–2003) stood out as a world-class intellectual who was born in Jerusalem and educated at both Princeton and Harvard. He was globally renowned in the fields of literary criticism and comparative literature, and was a political activist and advocate for Palestinian rights. In 1992 he attained the rank of university professor, Columbia University's most prestigious academic position. Professor Said also taught at Johns Hopkins, Yale, and Harvard. He was fluent in English, French, and Arabic. In 1999 Said served as president of the Modern Language Association.

In the computer industry, Dr. Taher Elgamal (1955–), an Egyptian cryptographer, served as chief scientist at Netscape Communications from 1995 to 1998. Steven Paul Jobs (1955–) was born in the United States, but his father was from Syria. Jobs has served as the co-founder, chairman, and CEO of Apple Inc. and is a former CEO of Pixar Animation Studios. Jobs resigned from Apple and founded NeXT, a computer platform development company specializing in the higher education and business markets. NeXT's subsequent 1997 buyout by Apple Computer Inc. brought Jobs back to the company he co-founded, and he returned to his position as CEO.

During the 1990s Dr. Dean Ahmad (1948–) participated in Maryland and national Libertarian Party activities, including as platform committee chair and member of the judiciary committee. Born at sea as his mother fled from Palestine, Ahmad was raised in Pennsylvania and earned a bachelor's degree from Harvard University (1970) and a doctoral degree in astronomy and astrophysics from the University of Arizona (1975). Dr. Ahmad teaches religion and science at the University of Maryland, College Park.

Elias A. Zerhouni (1951–) was a consultant to the White House in 1985 under President Ronald Reagan and to the World Health Organization in 1988, when he returned to Johns Hopkins as director of the MRI division. He was appointed full professor in 1992, becoming the chairman of the radiology department in January 1996. Donna Edna Shalala (1941–   ) has served as president of the University of Miami, a private university in Coral Gables, Florida, since 2001. Prior to this appointment, she served for eight years as secretary of Health and Human Services under President Clinton. She was awarded the Presidential Medal of Freedom, the nation's highest civilian honor.

ECONOMICS, EMPLOYMENT, AND SOCIAL STATUS

Arab Americans managed to do well in many areas of American life in the 1990s. They typically preferred not to receive welfare or ask for assistance. They commonly started their own businesses and worked very hard to develop them. Approximately 42 percent of Arab Americans 16 years and older were in professional, management, or related occupations, as compared to 34 percent of the general U.S. population. Thirty percent of Arab Americans worked in sales and office occupations. Arab Americans also had a slightly lower unemployment rate. Eighty-four percent of Arab Americans under the age of 25 had high school diplomas, as compared to 80 percent of the total U.S. population, and 41 percent had at least their Bachelor's degree, as compared to 24 percent of the total U.S. population. About twice as many Arab Americans held a post-graduate degree (17 percent) as compared with other Americans in general (9 percent). In addition, more than half of the Arab ancestry population was bilingual, providing an advantage in the job market. Thus, educational achievement and occupational mobility resulted in higher-than-average incomes for Arab Americans. In 1999 Arab-American men working full-time and year-round had overall median earnings of $41,700, higher than the national average of $37,100. The level for Arab-American women was also higher than

Both male and female Arab Americans earned higher-than-average incomes, and as many as 42 percent were in management or the professions in the 1990s.

that of the national median, $31,800 as compared with $27,200. The highest earners were Lebanese men at $49,100, and Egyptian women at $35,200 per year. The lowest Arab-American earners were Moroccan men at $32,800, and Moroccan women at $27,100 per year.

Along with the upward mobility and strides made by Arab Americans came the flip side of poverty and need, especially in light of the Gulf War in Iraq and other upheavals in the Arab world. Approximately 17 percent of Arab Americans were in poverty in 1999, as compared to 12 percent of the total population. Most of those below the poverty threshold were Iraqis, as compared to 11 percent of Lebanese and Syrians. Iraqi children were the most likely to be living below the poverty line (41 percent), as compared to Lebanese children (15 percent).

A number of social service and charitable agencies, such as the Arab-American Family Support Center (AAFSC) in New York, addressed the needs of the indigent within the Arab-American community. These agencies assisted families with the stress of being immigrants with poor English skills, students without family in an unfamiliar land, or individuals with medical problems or mental health issues.

ASSIMILATION

In the early part of the 20th century, Arab Americans were able to assimilate into American society with relative ease. But as time progressed and their personas were increasingly vilified in the news, in movies, on television, in books, and in conversations, some Arab Americans experienced cultural marginalization and began to live on the border of the American experience. Because of their culture and beliefs, and the way that others saw them, they began to feel like outsiders within their new country. According to scholar Nabeel Abraham, they coped with such marginalization in one of three ways: denying their ethnic identity; withdrawing into their own ethnic enclave; or engaging mainstream society head-on through information campaigns aimed at the news media, book publishers, politicians, and schools.

In the first instance, changing their Arabic names, never mentioning their Arab ancestry, or denying it completely was a way of assimilating into the American society at large and avoiding the curiosity of others or being stereotyped. Choosing to interact almost exclusively with those of the same ethnic group contributed to Arab Americans' marginalization and isolation within American society. This became increasingly easy to do, as Arab Americans usually lived in clusters or neighborhoods, or at least kept in close contact with members of their own ethnic group or had their own grocery stores and mosques.

In some instances, Arab Americans had their own schools, newspapers in Arabic, many places of business, and a growing number of social and political organizations. As Arab culture is traditionally very nurturing as well as protective of the members of its group, especially the women, it was quite easy to be insulated and interact solely with the family or members of the group. Speaking Arabic also aided in this "separateness." Such chosen isolation further marginalized them from participating fully as Americans.

Those who chose the third approach of campaigning through news media, books, publishers, politicians, and schools, seemed most balanced in their approach to life as American citizens. Their choice was considered keeping the best of both worlds—Arab and American—but often at a cost of constant campaigning, advocacy, and educating others about their identity. Such campaigning involved professional, educational, community, and cultural exchanges, mainly seeking to strike a balance between two different worlds and to have the larger American society better understand and appreciate the Arab world. Having their own language, Arabic, had much to do with their ability to balance between these two worlds. Arab professionals who worked outside of the group, or their children who went to public schools, were more likely to speak English away from home and Arabic when they returned home.

Americans who were not Arab had less of an opportunity to understand Islam, because unless one was a Muslim, they could not be initiated into the

Women and children at a community Ramadan retreat in Gloucester, Massachusetts. Like many other ethnic groups in the United States, Arab Americans relied on tight-knit community groups that sometimes had the potential for self-segregation and isolation from the larger culture.

The Islamic Society of Northern Wisconsin transformed this former Lutheran church in Altoona, Wisconsin, into a mosque in 1992. It now serves 40 families while hosting regular visitors from local schools and universities as a way to interact with the community.

inner community of the religion and its traditions, or even to interact with members of the group on a wider scale, including both genders. In spite of the many efforts to bridge gaps of understanding and to facilitate friendly inter-action, stereotypes persisted. One of the stereotypes was that all Arabs were money-hungry oil sheiks or profiteers, responsible for the increase in gasoline prices. Other stereotypes prevalent during the 1990s included perceptions of Arab men as irrational, morally inferior, barbaric, unclean, and abusive to their women. Arab women were labeled as passive, victimized, and submis-sive, or as belly-dancing harem girls. Both men and women were stereotyped as supporters of terrorism, although they were also the targets of sporadic, intentional violence and hate crimes.

Painting a picture of Arabs in these negative ways resulted in mistrust from the larger society and kept Arabs out of the political realms where change and full partnership with others could flourish. As with other ethnic groups, such as African Americans, Latinos, and other immigrants, such stereotyping served to exclude a people from sharing in the ideals, hopes, and resources of the American dream.

Muslim women have had to counter many stereotypes in American culture. This Muslim woman wears traditional dress on an American city street while using a cell phone.

Before the Arab-Israeli War of 1967, pre–World War II Arab immigrants to the United States and more recent, post–World War II Arab immigrants found it difficult to understand each others' concerns. The pre–World War II immigrants preferred to not seriously challenge U.S. views on Arab issues. But after 1967, both groups perceived a general American hostility toward Arabs, which drew the two groups closer together. By the 1980s, the majority of Arab Americans avoided involvement in politics, forming immigrant aid and cultural societies, rather than political organizations. They were interested in the events in their home countries, and deeply affected by the often-unsettling politics and events of the Middle East as described in the media. In the early 20th century they endured the racism that denied them American citizenship, and fought back. In more contemporary times, however, they struggled against a newer, more insidious stereotyping that painted them as undesirables and terrorists. To counter this, they found it necessary to gradually develop their own media and information systems, striving to provide what was considered to be unbiased accounts of the involvements and concerns of Arabs locally and around the world.

ARAB MEDIA IN THE 1990s

A few national bilingual publications (Arabic-English) were produced in the United States in the 1990s. *Jusoor* ("Bridges"), first published in 1992, included poetry and essays on politics and the arts. In 1996 the periodical *Al-Nashra* was first published. However, Arab Americans sought new media to cover serious issues and current events. Al Jazeera served that purpose.

Al Jazeera, which means "the island," is the largest Arabic news channel in the Middle East, offering Arabic programming and news coverage from around the world, 24 hours a day. The reporting focuses on regions of conflict, providing graphic and raw news coverage, and the network has received criticism from some governments around the world. Based in Qatar, it was founded in 1996 and became the fastest-growing network of its kind among Arab communities and Arabic-speaking people around the world. The station drew a large audience, which was largely accustomed to government-imposed censorship and biased coverage and saw credibility in Al Jazeera. Much of the Arab-American audience was glad to receive news coverage by an Arabic news channel that they could compare and cross-reference to the news coverage by the American media, which they often believed was biased.

RACIAL IDENTITY AND DISCRIMINATION

Like Latin Americans, Arab Americans are a part of a multiracial (although "race" is a social construct), multilinguistic, and multireligious group. Although from a variety of geographical backgrounds, they were often seen as one distinct category in the United States. Arabs were classified as white by most definitions, but in popular discourse, they were also different from and inferior to mainstream white America. They were considered "white, but not quite," or viewed as "others." Arab-American skin colors vary from very pale to dark, as do their eye colors, and those with darker complexions were often treated differently.

A correspondent for the English version of Al Jazeera conducts an interview at the Pentagon with Chairman of the Joint Chiefs of Staff Mike Mullen on July 2, 2009. Al Jazeera has continued to draw a large Arab-American audience since it began broadcasting in the late 1990s.

A controversial change in U.S. census reporting categories came in 1997, when the Office of Management and Budget (OMB) Statistical Policy Directive No. 15, Race and Ethnic Standards for Federal Statistics and Administrative Reporting, listed the category of "white" as "a person having origins in any of the original peoples of Europe, North Africa, or the Middle East." Within the same report it is noted: "No research has been conducted on the quality and consistency of reporting of persons of Arab or Middle Eastern descent on the race item on previous decennial censuses. Directive No. 15 instructs persons of Middle Eastern or North African descent to report their race as 'White.' However, it is not known how well this instruction is followed—or even if persons know that such a definition exists. Over the years there has been confusion about how persons of these ancestries should respond—'Asian,' 'White,' or 'Other race.' Requests for consideration of adding an Arab or Middle Eastern category have not been consistent in the suggested name and the criteria for the definition of what geographic area should be encompassed."

As in many other countries and cultures, a historical pattern of discrimination persisted in 1990s America against people of color. In his book *Racist America*, Joe Feagin writes that whites in the United States have most often judged newcomers along a "white-to-black status continuum." Those closest to white were considered more civilized, and those who were dark were considered less civilized. This continuum is expanded, adding the characteristic of "foreignness." Hence, groups are also judged on how "foreign" they seem—which might also be signaled by accent, clothing, food, and various home country traditions. This suggests that Arab Americans have been judged not only in terms of their fit along the white-black continuum, but also for their degree of "foreignness."

One of the interesting consequences of the difficulty of assimilation was a growing identification with others who were faced with the same dilemma. According to Helen Hatab Samhan, Executive Director of the Arab American Institute

A Sudanese Muslim man praying. In the 1990s the number of Muslims from Africa and North Africa increased in the U.S. population.

Arab-American Music and Film

Thriving art communities were developed by Arab Americans in many cities in America, which continued throughout the 1990s. For instance, the "Electric Arab Orchestra" entertained in Minneapolis, Minnesota with an exciting blend of Arabian and rock music. National and international music had its appeal within Arab-American communities. Musical groups like Nass El Ghiwane from Morocco, which began playing in the 1960s, increased their appeal in the 1990s due to their poetry set to music, and their conveyance of the social and political climate of a people. Musicians like Sheikh Imam of Egypt also brought political awareness. However, the newer musicians found an audience that was ready to hear contemporary issues addressed.

Arab-American film also won more attention during the 1990s. In California's San Francisco Bay area, Arab Americans founded the Bay Area Arab Film Festival in 1997 with the purpose of promoting Arab and Arab-American cinema and films. By featuring such films, the festival also furthers understanding of Arab cultures and works against stereotypes of Arabs in mainstream film in the United States.

Foundation in Washington D.C., there was a trend toward pan-ethnic identities, which was more prevalent among U.S.-born Arabs. Arab Americans were identifying themselves more and more as being of Arab descent rather than by country of origin. This provided more fertile ground for unified Arab-American political, cultural, and social organizational efforts. Also, Arab Americans from North Africa—Muslim and non-Muslim—were increasing in number, and were sharing concerns with other Arab Americans as well as with African Americans.

POLITICAL TENSIONS

Increasingly in the 1990s, Arab Americans began to identify themselves as Arab to non-Arabs, and less as representatives of the separate nations from which they or their parents originated. Within the 1990s there grew a sense of distrust by Arab Americans over what they perceived as America's unfair favoring of Israel over Palestine or any other Arab nation. Political tensions increased and social relations between Arabs and non-Arab groups were further strained.

On January 16, 1991, the United States, along with a large international coalition backed by the United Nations, launched an offensive against Iraqi forces in occupation of Kuwait, beginning the Gulf War. Before this offensive move, Iraq had been considered an ally of the United States, especially during the war between Iraq and Iran. But faced with economic disaster after that war, Iraq's president, Saddam Hussein, decided to invade Kuwait, its other neighbor. U.S. President George H.W. Bush quickly moved to intervene, and Iraqi forces suffered heavy casualties and retreated after they were attacked. A cease-fire was declared on February 8, 1991. Heavy sanctions were imposed upon Iraq.

This conflict between the United States and a Middle Eastern country fueled the fire of hate crimes in America against Arab Americans, or those who were perceived to be Arab American. Crimes such as vandalism, harassment, assault, and death threats, which had existed prior to the conflict, increased. While the FBI warned Arab Americans of the possibility of backlash after this first Gulf War, Arab-Americans were at the same time assessed for terrorist potential. In a 1991 opinion poll, about 60 percent of Americans attributed the characteristics of "terrorists" and "violent" to Arabs.

CONCLUSION

Another event in the early 1990s had a significant impact on the perception of Arab Americans. On February 26, 1993, extremists detonated a bomb in the parking garage of One World Trade Center in New York City, killing six people and injuring hundreds of others. In 1994 four Arab and Muslim suspects were tried, each receiving prison sentences of 240 years. In 1996, 10 additional Muslim fundamentalists were convicted. Their sentences ranged from 25 years, to life imprisonment. Arab-American fears of backlash increased after these events. The government and media did, however, portray the bombing as the work of fanatics, who were different than most law-abiding Arab Americans. In the next decade, this bombing would be revisited on a much larger scale after the attacks of September 11, 2001.

DENISE HINDS-ZAAMI
PENNSYLVANIA STATE UNIVERSITY

Further Reading

Abraham, Sameer Y., ed, and Nabeel Abraham. *The Arab World and Arab-Americans: Understanding a Neglected Minority.* Detroit, MI: Wayne State University Center for Urban Studies, 1981.
———. *Arabs in the New World. Studies on Arab-American Communities.* Detroit, MI: Wayne State University Center for Urban Studies, 1983.
Allied Media Corp. *Multicultural Communication.* Available online, URL: www.allied-media.com. Accessed December 18, 2008.

Arab American National Museum. Available online, URL: www.Arab
    AmericanMuseum.org. Accessed December 18, 2008.
De la Cruz, Patricia G. and Angela Brittingham. *The Arab Population: 2000.*
    United States Census 2000, December 2003. Available online, URL:
    www.census.gov. Accessed December 18, 2008.
Feagin, Joe R. *Racist America: Roots, Current Realities and Future Repara-*
    tions. Lanham, MD: Routledge, 2000.
Haiek, Joseph R. *Arab-American Almanac.* 4th ed. Glendale, CA: News
    Circle, 1992.
Jamal, Amaney, ed. and Nadine Naber. *Race and Arab Americans Before*
    and After 9/11. From Invisible Citizens to Visible Subjects. Syracuse,
    NY: Syracuse University, 2008.
Kayyali, Randa A. *The Arab Americans. The New Americans.* Westport, CT:
    Greenwood, 2006.
Marvasti, Amir and Karyn D. McKinney. *Middle Eastern Lives in America.*
    Lanham, MD: Rowman & Littlefield, 2004.
Middle East News and World Report. *Introduction to the Arab World.* "The
    Great History of the Arab People and Civilization." Available online,
    URL: www.middleeastnews.com. Accessed November 16, 2008.
Samhan, Helen Hatab. "By the Numbers." *Arab American Market.* Allied
    Media Corp. Available online, URL: www.allied-media.com/Arab
    -American/Arab_demographics.htm. Accessed November 21, 2008.
Shaheen, Jack. *Reel Bad Arabs: How Hollywood Vilifies a People,* 2nd ed.
    New York: Olive Branch Press, 2009.
Shakir, Evelyn. *Bint Arab. Arab and Arab American Women in the United*
    States. Westport, CT: Praeger, 1997.
Suleiman, Michael W., ed. *Arabs in America: Building a New Future.* Phila-
    delphia, PA: Temple University, 1999.
Zogby, Dr. James. *Are Arab Americans People Like Us?* Arab American Insti-
    tute. Available online, URL: www.aaiusa.org/dr-zogby/356/people
    -like-us. Accessed December 1, 2000.

CHAPTER 10

The 21st Century: 2000 to the Present

THERE WERE 1.2 million people of Arab ancestry living in the United States in 2000, according to the U.S. Census Bureau. That number grew from 610,000 in 1980, when Arab Americans were first identified as a distinct element of the American population, to 860,000 in 1990. Those with roots in Egypt made up the fastest-growing group within the Arab-American population. This group swelled from 79,000 in 1990 to 143,000 in 2000. Three-fifths of Arab Americans report that their ancestors were born in Lebanon (37 percent), Egypt (12 percent), or Syria (12 percent). Other frequently cited countries of origin include Palestine, Jordan, Morocco, and Iraq. More than four percent of Arab Americans record their ancestry as Yemeni, Kurdish, Algerian, Saudi Arabian, Tunisian, Kuwaiti, Libyan, or Berber.

In the decade preceding 2000, the population of Arab Americans grew in virtually every state in the Union. California witnessed the largest growth, expanding by 48,000. Michigan and Florida saw increases of 39,000 and 28,000, respectively. Arab Americans tend to cluster in urban areas spread throughout the United States. There are large Arab-American communities in Los Angeles, Detroit, New York City, Chicago, and Washington, D.C. Two-thirds of all Arab Americans live in only 10 states, with one-third living in California, New York, and Michigan. Most Arab Americans are not immigrants. They were born in the United States, and their families may

143

have been in residence for many generations. While they have become assimilated into American society over time, Arab Americans tend to retain certain cultural traditions that reflect their unique heritages. Understanding this culture is made more difficult because of the scarcity of a viable body of academic literature on Arab Americans.

Even though most Arab Americans are not Muslims, they are often assumed to hold the same belief systems as adherents of Islam. Scholars contend that there is no valid record of the number of Muslims in the United States; estimates range widely between two and almost six million. Since the 1990s Muslims residing in the United States have often been looked upon with suspicion, which has sometimes been spurred on by the media. When a disgruntled U.S. Navy veteran bombed the Alfred P. Murrah Federal Building in Oklahoma City on April 19, 1995, killing 168 people, some members of the media immediately jumped to the conclusion that the attack had been carried out by Arab terrorists, as did some of the American public. When such an attack did occur on September 11, 2001, many felt justified for their earlier suspicions. Innocent Arab Americans, many of whom felt just as betrayed as other Americans by the 9/11 attacks, became the victims of overt discrimination, as well as physical and personal attacks.

IMMIGRATION AND DEMOGRAPHICS

The Asia Exclusion Act was repealed in 1965, precipitating a new wave of Arab immigration into the United States. These new immigrants were more diverse than those who had preceded them. Two major Islamic organizations were founded to serve the needs of the vast Arab-American population. The Muslim World League (MWL) and the Organization of Islamic Conference (OIC) were subsequently recognized by the federal government as viable nongovernmental organizations (NGOs), with the right to appoint diplomats to represent their interests. The last decade of the 20th century witnessed a new surge of Arab immigration into the United States in response to the Gulf War, and the subsequent withdrawal of support by Saudi Arabia and other nations in the Persian Gulf. A more tolerant view of Arab-American culture evolved during the Clinton administration (1992–2000). In 1986 there were 598 mosques in the United States. By 2000 that number had grown to 1,200. During the same period, more than 200 Islamic schools were established throughout the country.

Arab-American scholars frequently lament the fact that the term "Arab American" has been used to describe a large group of individuals with diverse languages, national origins, ethnicities, religious beliefs, and cultural traditions. Individuals identified as Arab Americans have emigrated from one of 26 Arab-speaking nations of the world. More than half of all Arab Americans living in the United States in the early 21st century were born in the United States. Many of those families could trace their roots to Arab Americans who

New immigration patterns have increased the number of Muslims in the United States and altered the population of cities such as Fargo, North Dakota. This Federal Emergency Management Agency (FEMA) staffer furnished an Arabic-speaking city resident with information in his native language during a flood emergency on June 18, 2009.

had been in the United States for many generations. Approximately 82 percent of all Arab Americans are U.S. citizens.

When compared to the general adult population, Arab Americans tend to be younger and better educated. They are also more likely to participate in the labor force and to earn higher incomes. Approximately 58 percent of adult Arab Americans are engaged in managerial, professional, technical, sales, and administration positions, as compared to only 43 percent of the general adult population.

Unlike Arab Americans who have been in the United States for generations, almost all immigrant Muslims send money back to their homelands to help support family members. The Muslim faith requires its members to be actively involved in charity work, and Arab Americans who are Muslims tend to donate large sums of money to support poor widows and orphans. It was this practice that allowed Arab terrorists to use legitimate charities to fund terrorist activities. Since the attacks of September 11, 2001, Arab-American donations to charities have been closely monitored.

The difference in the demographics of Arab Americans and other Americans is chiefly a response to changes in patterns of immigration. After World War II, many Arab-American immigrants relocated to the United States as a result of political unrest in their home countries. Most of these immigrants come from middle- and upper-class backgrounds, and, unlike other groups of Arab Americans, three-fourths of the more recent immigrants are practicing Muslims.

While non-Arabs sometimes lump together all groups within the Arab-American community, there are other distinct differences according to national origin, language, religion, political orientation, and time spent in the United States. Sudanese Muslims, for instance, are rarely political. The majority of this group came to the United States to study medicine, finance, computer science, management, and engineering. Rather than attempting to assimilate into American culture, many traditional Muslim immigrants find American society decadent. They believe that alcohol consumption, drug addiction, nudity on television and in movies, and the prevalence of sex outside marriage are indica-

Arab-American Cuisine in the Southwest

When people of Arab-American descent meet one another, they may ask *¿Eres paisano*, meaning, "Are you a country man?" An affirmative answer is likely to precipitate a bonding experience in which food plays a large part. The desert culture that originated with the ancestors of Arab Americans is still very much alive in cities such as the former mining city of Ajo, Arizona. Patrons of Arab-American restaurants in Ajo may enjoy *jocoque*, a refreshing yogurt-like drink that is ideal in the arid climate. Other menu choices include *hojas de vid* (stuffed grapes), *berenjena asada* (grilled eggplant), *jumus bi-tajin con limón* (mashed chickpeas combined with sesame paste and lime juice), *eftoyer* (triangular pies made of spinach), and *quebbe* (a dish of ground lamb to which onions, bulgur wheat, and piñon nuts are added). Dishes concocted with *mole poblano* sauce (guacamole, for instance), *chiles en nogadas* (chili with walnuts), and *motuleños* (eggs with black beans, cheese, and other ingredients) combine Arabic cuisine with that of the Americas to produce widely popular dishes that are frequently identified with Mexican cuisine.

Salty cheese made from the milk of goats and sheep is a staple in many Arab-American homes, and is used to season a variety of dishes. More familiar foods served in the homes of Arab Americans who come from desert backgrounds include dates, figs, olives, apricots, grapes, pomegranates, citrus fruits, lentils, peas, chickpeas, okra, cucumber, melon, and garlic. Certain Arabian spices are imported because they have no equivalent in the United States, but some enterprising Arab-American cooks have used pine nuts, oregano, mints, and sumac berries as substitutes for Arab seasonings that are not easy to find. Restaurants serving traditional foods that originated in the deserts of the Middle East are located in El Paso, Mexicali, Laredo, Ajo, and other towns along the border of the United States and Mexico.

Muslim women praying during the Eid holiday in Roxbury, Massachusetts, in 2007. About 75 percent of recent Arab immigrants to the United States have been Muslim.

tions that the global power of the United States is on the wane. Other Arab immigrants, such as earlier non-Muslim arrivals, are often more assimilated and may not share these views.

FAMILY AND CULTURE

While many Arab-American children have become assimilated, there are inherent differences in the cultures practiced within traditionally Arabic homes and communities and those of other Americans. Arab children are taught that well-behaved children bring honor to their families, while those who misbehave bring dishonor; they are also brought up to exhibit great respect for their elders. They learn to shake hands with all visitors, and when guests are family or friends, they greet them with kisses. Arab children often refer to adults they know well by courtesy titles such as "aunt" and "uncle." Physical punishment is rarely used in Arab-American families, as most parents prefer to use shaming as a disciplinary tool. Islamic law identifies classes of behavior, and obeying adults is required of all Muslim children. It is unacceptable for children in Muslim families to question the dictates of their parents, or to refuse to perform assigned tasks within the household. It is also understood that Arab-American children will work in family-owned businesses, on the assumption that it builds character and fosters a sense of responsibility.

Children are considered great assets in Arabic families, particularly among Muslim families. This young girl was waiting for Eid prayers to begin in Roxbury, Massachusetts, in 2007.

Arab men are considered the heads of their families and have complete control over decision making. Consequently, Arab women are often stereotypically portrayed as excessively modest and submissive, and are accused of hiding behind traditional veils. While it is true that Arab women are bound by certain cultural dictates such as remaining virgins until they marry and fulfilling traditional roles as wives and mothers, Arab-American women have taken an active role in reshaping perceptions of Arab Americans since the September 11, 2001, terrorist attacks that forced Arab-American men to adopt lower profiles. On the other hand, Arab-American women are less likely to participate in the labor force (59.9 percent) than white Americans (73.2 percent). Just over 84 percent of Arab immigrant females are able to speak English when they arrive in the United States, and over three-fourths have been in the country for more than five years. Approximately 27 percent have at least a bachelor's degree.

Traditional Arab Americans often participate in arranged marriages as a means of preserving ethnicity and religious integrity. This practice has led many Arab-American males to import brides from their homelands. As a result, some couples do not meet until the marriage takes place. Romantic love is considered not nearly as important as status and security. When young Arab Americans want to marry a particular person, they seek parental approval. Among the approximately 40,000 Somalis who have immigrated to the United States, arranged marriages among members of the same clan are generally the norm. In addition to nuclear families, the Arab-American family includes extended family members, and it is expected that grown children will care for aging parents.

RELIGION

Contrary to popular opinion, not all Arab Americans are Muslim. Two-thirds of this population is Christian. Those who endorse Islam are divided into Sunni, Shia, Druze, and other minority sects. There are several million Muslims in the United States, and nearly 70 percent of them were born in America. Around 30 percent of Muslims are American-born African Americans who have converted to Islam, and have no direct link to Arab-speaking countries. Another third of the American Muslim population hails from South Asia. There is a good deal of controversy over perceived goals of Muslim Arab Americans. Rather than endorsing the notion that the United States is an "evil empire" out to destroy Islam, most Arab-American Muslims have been assimilated into American culture. Most observant American Muslims do, however, continue to plan their daily lives around designated prayer times.

Arab Americans who are Muslims celebrate Ramadan, which falls in the ninth month of the Muslim calendar. Ramadan calls for participation in a month of fasting and restraint. According to Muslim belief, the holiday celebrates the

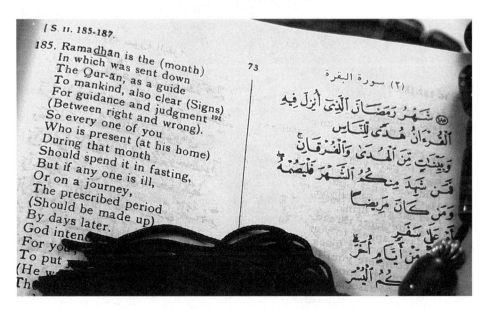

A page of the Qur'an describing the month of fasting during Ramadan. At the end of the month, Muslims gather for three days of celebrations of the Feast of Fast Breaking.

delivery of the Qur'an as a guide to the Islamic faith. Thus, Ramadan is a time of great religious significance and social interaction with other Muslims. It is considered particularly offensive for Muslims to tell lies, gossip, or be greedy during Ramadan. Muslims are required to pray to Allah five times each day facing toward the Holy City of Mecca. During Ramadan a lengthy night prayer is added. At the end of the month of fasting, Muslims celebrate the Feast of Fast Breaking by gathering together with friends and family for three days and exchanging gifts. At the end of Ramadan, Muslims also pay *zakat,* a kind of tax that is given to the needy and intended as a purification of accumulated wealth.

POLITICS

While many people believe that all Arabs and Muslims are ideologically in tune, this is far from the truth. In the 21st century, there has been an increasingly widening chasm between newer immigrants and those who have been in the United States for generations, which has arisen due to differences on certain issues, particularly on foreign policy affairs concerning Arab countries. Politically, Arab Americans may be Democrats, Republicans, or Independents. Far from being radically fundamentalist on political issues, many Arab Americans take no interest in politics at all.

The estimated 1.5 million Arab-American voters in Michigan, Ohio, Florida, and Pennsylvania form a significant voting bloc during presidential elections in these crucial states. This woman was at work on a voter petition in Somerville, Massachusetts, in 2007.

"Honor" Killings

Because males in traditional Muslim families have almost total control over their female family members, some Muslims believe they have the right to kill female relatives who disobey or who are considered to have brought dishonor on the family name. To date, "honor" killings have been reported in Bangladesh, Britain, Brazil, Ecuador, Egypt, India, Israel, Italy, Jordan, Morocco, Sweden, Syria, Turkey, Uganda, the United States, Afghanistan, Iraq, and Iran. Honor killings are particularly prevalent in Pakistan, where the notion of women as property is entrenched in society.

The most cited reason for honor killings is that daughters have refused to marry individuals chosen by their parents. Other grounds for murdering Arab females include being the victim of a sexual assault, being involved in a divorce, engaging in adultery or sexual intercourse outside of marriage, flirting, or receiving telephone calls from men.

Despite global protests against the practice, honor killings continue to occur among Arab families, including in the United States. On November 6, 1989, Zein Isa, the father of a Palestinian family living in St. Louis, stabbed his 16-year-old daughter Palestina (Tina) to death because she had taken a part-time job and was dating an African American.

Isa was not a typical Arab-American parent. He was involved with the Abu Idal Organization that was under investigation for plotting to bomb the Israeli Embassy in Washington, D.C. Because he was under FBI surveillance in 1989, the murder of Palestina Isa was recorded on tape. This action negated Isa's claim of self defense and supported the contention that Isa's Brazilian-born wife Maria had been involved in her daughter's murder.

Some Arab-American leaders have launched campaigns to encourage greater political participation in the Arab-American community. In Dearborn, Michigan, leaders have launched the "One Voice" campaign to register Arab-American voters and promote enhanced interest in issues that directly affect daily life and well-being. Another goal of the program is to force Democratic and Republican presidential candidates to pay attention to the concerns of Arab Americans.

During the 2000 election, Arab Americans were more likely to support Republican candidate George W. Bush, who had met with Arab-American leaders in the course of his campaign. During the presidential debates, Bush expressed qualms about the practice of profiling Arabs and Muslims, which had been used since the Oklahoma City bombing of 1995, even though that attack was perpetrated by an American.

Tony Shalhoub

In the 1990s and 2000s, Arab Americans achieved significant success in the mainstream entertainment industry. One of the most popular Arab-American entertainers is Tony Shalhoub, who stars in the USA channel's popular series *Monk*, which is about a San Francisco–based former police detective with obsessive-compulsive disorder. He became a private detective and police consultant after a breakdown forced him off the police force following his wife's murder. The show's theme song, written and sung by Randy Newman, describes an obsessive-compulsive's world besieged by hidden terrors, and also mirrors a new consciousness about threats to the environment:

> *It's a jungle out there*
> *Poison in the very air we breathe*
> *Do you know what's in the water that you drink?*
> *Well I do, and it's amazing.*

Tony Shalhoub was born in Green Bay, Wisconsin, in 1953 to a Lebanese immigrant father and a second-generation Lebanese-American mother. Shalhoub first achieved success in 1990 when he joined the cast of *Wings*, playing Italian taxi driver Antonio Scarpacci. He used this success as a vehicle to launch a film career, appearing in such blockbusters as *Men in Black* (1997) and *Men in Black II* (2002) with Will Smith and Tommy Lee Jones. Shalhoub appealed to younger fans as the voice of Luigi in Pixar Animation's *Cars* in 2006, and in the *Spy Kids* series and games based on that series. He also played in less commercial films such as *Primary Colors, The Siege,* and *A Civil Action,* all in 1998, as well as *Galaxy Quest* (1999), *Thirteen Ghosts* (2001), and the award-winning *The Man Who Wasn't There* (2001).

Shalhoub, who is married to actress Brooke Adams, long ago won the respect of critics and fans alike with his varied career, but it was not until he accepted the role of Adrian Monk that Shalhoub became a household name and helped to bring other Arab-American entertainers into the mainstream of American entertainment. Shalhoub's portrayal of Monk netted him four straight Emmy Awards as Outstanding Lead Actor in a Comedy Series between 2003 and 2006. In addition to the Emmy Awards, Shalhoub, who is also the executive producer of *Monk*, has been recognized by the American Film Institute, the Golden Globe Association, the Screen Actors Guild, the Chicago Film Critics Association, the Family Television Awards, the Independent Spirit Awards, the National Society of Film Critics, the Northampton Film Festival, the Online Film Critics Society, the Prism Awards, and the Television Critics Association.

A plurality of some 44.5 percent of Arab-American voters supported George Bush in 2000, but that support had declined to 28 percent by 2004. This decline in loyalties to Bush was largely due to the war in Iraq. Polls also repeatedly mirrored the dissatisfaction of Arab-American voters who took the Republican administration to task for discriminating against Arabs and Muslims, violating civil liberties since the passage of the Patriot Act, mishandling the war in Iraq, and continuing to support Israel. In the key states of Michigan, Ohio, Florida, and Pennsylvania, there are perhaps more than 1.5 million Arab Americans who could play a large part in determining the outcome of any presidential election, especially if either of the major parties were particularly vulnerable. Arab Americans favored Barack Obama over John McCain by 54 percent to 33 percent in a poll taken before the 2008 election.

IMPACT OF 9/11

Toward the end of the 20th century, Arabs and Muslims living in the United States, particularly those who were not citizens, became suspect because of various terrorist acts. Beginning in the 1970s a number of congressional acts and executive regulations made it possible for investigators to selectively target Arab immigrants for intense questioning and possible deportation. The suspicion of Muslims heightened with the outbreak of the Iranian Revolution and the taking of American hostages in Iran in 1979. Even greater attention was paid to Arab Americans after the fall of the Soviet Union, when Arab terrorists were identified as the major remaining threat to American national security.

Anxious to strike out at someone, a number of Americans became openly hostile to all Arab Americans after the attacks of September 11, 2001, when terrorists hijacked four large passenger jets and used them to attack the World Trade Center in New York and the Pentagon in Washington, D.C. A fourth attack was thwarted by passengers on United Flight 93 when the plane was forced into the ground in Shanksville, Pennsylvania. Nearly 3,000 people lost their lives on 9/11, including the terrorists, and hundreds of others became ill after working to clean up the aftermath of the two attacks on the World Trade Center.

As a result of the 9/11 attacks, Arab Americans, particularly those who are Muslims, have often been unfairly linked with terrorism. Some scholars suggest that Islam and Muslims have been "demonized" in popular fiction since 9/11. They contend that law-abiding, Arab-American citizens have been labeled "radical" and/or "extremist," and accuse President George W. Bush of contributing to the prevailing "us versus them" mentality. These scholars also maintain that the war on terrorism has become a war on Islam. Other scholars contend that this demonizing began long before 9/11. Jack Shaheen, for instance, spent four years studying the way that Arabs and Muslims were portrayed in 900 films. He concluded that the movie industry had vilified

Letter from an Arab American

A week after 9/11, an Arab American wrote the following letter to President George W. Bush. Bush had spoken at the Islamic Center in Washington, D.C., the day before. Noting that "America counts millions of Muslims amongst our citizens, and Muslims make an incredibly valuable contribution to our country," Bush urged Americans to not take out their rage over 9/11 on the Arab-American community.

Date: 09/18/2001 09:03 AM EDT
From: Sami
To: President George W. Bush
Subject: Peace

Dear Mr. President,

Your words at the Islamic Center in Washington D.C. have touched all Arab Americans and Muslim Americans. Thank you for standing out so strongly for the rights of all people in this nation regardless of color, race, creed or religion. You are a patriot of principles. We all stand with you in condemning this heinous crime against humanity.

Please accept our heartfelt sympathies and condolences. As a 2nd generation Arab-American family, we share and grieve with everyone. We all wake up everyday to go to work in order to provide for our loved ones. We all fly on planes as part of business or pleasure.

This is the American way of life, and we cherish it. The tragedy that befell all those who went to work that morning or who got onto an airplane touches each and everyone. Brooklyn is my place of birth, and New York City is one of mankind's greatest engineering marvels. The devastation brought on by such senseless and mad people is beyond comprehension.

The heinous act perpetrated on Sept. 11 is condemned in the strongest terms by people of all faiths and ethnic backgrounds. This is clearly a crime against humanity. May God bless you with all the strength and wisdom needed to carry this nation forward in these difficult times.

Salam, Peace, and Shalom,

Sami
Naperville, Illinois
2nd Generation Arab American

Visitors to the World Trade Center site reading a list of the victims of the attack just after the one-year anniversary of 9/11 in September 2002.

Arabs and Muslims by portraying them as one of five types: villains, sheikhs, maidens, Egyptians, or Palestinians. Arab women, he maintained, were seen as weak and mute. They were shown swathed in black clothing and veils or portrayed as almost nude belly dancers.

In the days after the Oklahoma City bombing in 1995, police officers reported 222 incidences of vandalism, harassment, and assault against Arab Americans. Such crimes were repeated in New York City and Washington, D.C. after the attacks on 9/11. Over the following week, assaults on Arab Americans spread to other cities. In Dallas, Texas, an attacker opened fire on a mosque. Officials closed public schools in New Orleans, Louisiana, because of threats to Arab and Muslim students. In Chicago, Illinois, a bomb was set off at an Arab-American community center. According to the Southern Poverty Law Center, threats and incidents were reported in 25 states and the nation's capital. The Council on American-Islamic Relations reported 411 separate threats to Arab and Muslim Americans. The FBI opened case files on 40 reported hate crimes. Three of those involved murder. The American Arab Anti-Discrimination Committee began receiving a slew of hate mail. Attacks were also perpetrated against those who were assumed to be Arab or Muslim. An Arizona man, Balbir Singh Sodhi, who had immigrated to the United States from India, was killed when he was mistaken for a Muslim.

THE PATRIOT ACT

The determination to prevent terrorists from attacking the United States again led Congress to pass the Uniting and Strengthening America by Providing Appropriate Tools Required to Intercept and Obstruct Terrorism Act, more commonly known as the USA Patriot Act (Public Law 107-56) 45 days after 9/11. The act gave the president of the United States virtually unlimited powers to fight terrorism. Only one senator and 66 representatives opposed the Patriot Act, which cleared the way for federal agents to arrest suspected terrorists and hold them indefinitely, including those who had no charges brought against them. It also allowed agents to monitor activities without prior notification. For the most part, the Arab-American community viewed the Patriot Act as a declaration of war on the constitutional protections of all Arabs and Muslims living in the United States.

Congress defined terrorism as virtually all actions that threatened human life. The stated purpose of the Patriot Act was "to deter and punish terrorist acts in the United States and around the world, to enhance law enforcement investigatory tools, and for other purposes." The law expressly condemned "discrimination against Arab and Muslim Americans." However, Arab and Muslim Americans became the major focus of suspicion because the profile of suspected terrorists focused on Arab immigrants and those of Arab descent. The federal government used the "authority to intercept wire, oral, and electronic communications relating to terrorism" granted in Section 201, Title II, to engage in what civil libertarians perceived as attacks on the constitutional rights of Arab and Muslim Americans. Federal officials were even allowed to monitor communications between lawyers and any clients who had come under suspicion. Communications with detainees in federal custody were also closely monitored.

Those who protested such high-handed federal actions maintained that the Patriot Act should not grant the federal government the right to place Arab Americans under surveillance without valid proof that they were connected to terrorism in some way. Some of the more controversial aspects of the law provided for "mandatory detention of suspected terrorists" and a suspension of habeas corpus and relaxed rules on obtaining search warrants. Federal officials were authorized to hold detainees for up to seven days without charging them, but Department of Justice regulations extended that time period indefinitely. Bush was harshly criticized for creating a military commission to conduct the trials of detainees suspected of being terrorists or of harboring suspected terrorists. There was also a good deal of discussion about allowing federal officials to use torture to force information from detainees, and Bush was severely criticized for creating his own definition of what constituted terrorism. Most of the controversial provisions of the bill were considered temporary, but in 2006 the Bush administration convinced Congress to make all but two provisions permanent.

President George W. Bush used the 9/11 attacks as justification for a number of actions that dismayed the Arab-American community. He is shown here speaking in August 2002 at the Department of Homeland Security in front of a depiction of a firefighter lost on 9/11.

With the support of Congress, federal officials used the Patriot Act and racial profiling to question 1,200 Arab and Muslim males about the attacks of 9/11 and uncover possible links to terrorism. Approximately 800 of the original 1,200 were immigrants. Officials also put together a list of 5,000 Arab and Muslim males to be brought in for voluntary questioning. A second list included an additional 3,000 individuals. Shortly thereafter, the State Department released information regarding new restrictions on the process of obtaining visas for all males between the ages of 16 and 45 from Arab and Muslim countries with known links to terrorism. The Immigration and Naturalization Service conducted a mass arrest of nonimmigrants from Syria, Pakistan, Libya, Saudi Arabia, Afghanistan, and Yemen, announcing that they had violated the terms of their visas. On December 6 Attorney General John Ashcroft announced that 6,000 Arab men were being detained as a result of ignoring deportation orders.

ENCOURAGING ASSIMILATION

American political and religious communities became actively involved in encouraging the assimilation of Arab Americans after 9/11. President Bush visited the Islamic Center in Washington, D.C., asserting that Islam was a religion of peace and that most Muslims were not engaged in terrorist acts.

The Guantánamo Detainees

In a number of high-profile cases after September 11, 2001, the U.S. government's actions toward a number of Arabs and Muslims, especially through detentions of suspected terrorists, have been challenged in federal courts. In 2002 President Bush established military camps at the Guantánamo Naval Base in Cuba. Approximately 800 detainees who were classified as "enemy combatants" were held in those facilities. To date, only a handful of detainees have officially been charged with a crime. Over 500 detainees have been released or transferred; some have been accused of engaging in terrorist activity after their release. Critics of the Bush administration claimed that Guantánamo detainees were consistently denied the right to communicate with legal counsel and were not allowed to maintain contact with their families. There were also claims of physical mistreatment amounting to torture.

The Bush administration repeatedly contended that Guanánamo detainees were exempt from the rules of the Geneva Convention, which has governed the treatment of prisoners of war since 1949. The Geneva Convention prohibits the following actions: "Violence to life and person, in particular murder of all kinds, mutilation, cruel treatment and torture; the taking of hostages; outrages upon personal dignity, in particular, humiliating and degrading treatment; the passing of sentences and the carrying out of executions without previous judgment pronounced by a regularly constituted court."

On June 29, 2008, the Supreme Court held in a 5-4 decision in *Boumediene v. Bush* (U.S. 06-1195) that Guantánamo detainees were protected by the U.S. Constitution and the Geneva Convention. Writing for a majority that included Justices John Paul Stevens, David Souter, Ruth Bader Ginsburg, and Steven Breyer, Justice Anthony Kennedy traced protections against illegal detainment back to the Magna Carta in 1215. The majority of the court held that the Detainee Treatment Act of 2005 had established inadequate provisions for determining the status of post-9/11 detainees, determining that those provisions were clearly not an "effective substitute for habeas corpus." Justice Antonin Scalia, a member of the dissenting minority, announced that the decision would likely "cause more Americans to be killed." The *Boumediene* decision also overturned the provision of the Military Commission Acts of 2006, which had prevented detainees from filing habeas corpus petitions in federal courts. The Bush administration subsequently announced that 60–90 Guantánamo detainees would be held for trial while others would be released.

On January 22, 2009, President Barack Obama issued an executive order that the Guantánamo detention camps were to be closed within one year. However, the administration encountered difficulty placing the detainees elsewhere because of diplomatic, legal, and political issues, and progress was slow. A year later Guantánamo was still holding detainees.

Christian and Jewish leaders stood outside mosques in the days following 9/11 to protect Arab Americans from attacks. Ordinary Americans also expressed their support for Arab Americans. Some American women wore scarves to demonstrate their solidarity with Arab-American women.

Conversely, many Arab-American women removed their veils to show that had been assimilated into American culture. Arab-American women also headed campaigns to raise money for the families of victims of 9/11 and sponsored blood drives. Suspicions were so strong against Arab-American males that some women suffered domestic violence in silence because they were reluctant to place their husbands in positions where they might be suspected of other crimes.

President Bush ordered American embassies to monitor the content of textbooks in Muslim countries so that any anti-American, anti-Western, or anti-Israeli content could be identified. Nongovernmental organizations, Muslim charities, and religious organizations were constantly monitored for potential links to terrorist organizations. In northern Virginia, federal agents conducted raids on homes and offices of leaders in the Muslim communities. Arab Americans reacted to unprovoked attacks in a variety of ways. Some enlisted in the U.S. military. Others offered to act as translators. Inside mosques, any literature that could be seen as promoting Islamic fundamentalism was

Arabs and Muslims in many fields have worked toward becoming better understood in U.S. culture. The photo shows Army Chaplain Abdul-Rasheed Muhammad, who became the first Muslim chaplain in the U.S. armed forces in 1994, during a promotion ceremony in June 2009.

quietly removed. Anxious not to offend, the owners of websites devoted to Arab Americans began engaging in self-censorship.

Between 2001 and 2006, the U.S. government detained more than 2,200 immigrants who were suspected of being in contact with known terrorists. Only four were officially charged with crimes, and two of those were acquitted when their cases went to trial. The states of Alaska, Hawaii, and Vermont and 140 American cities passed resolutions protesting the Patriot Act. Individuals throughout the United States lodged their own protests, which ranged from erasing Internet records on public computers, to refusing to release patient medical histories to government officials. Mary Rose Oakar, a former Democratic congresswoman from Ohio and the president of the American Arab Anti-Discrimination League, has been one of the most vocal opponents of the Patriot Act. She has stated repeatedly that the act is a denial of the Fourth Amendment's guarantee of protection from unreasonable search and seizure.

CONCLUSION

There have been positive developments for Arab Americans after 9/11 and in the late 2000s, as Arab Americans and sympathetic non-Arabs have come together to promote mutual understanding. Celebrations of Arab-American culture have been incorporated into the mainstream since 9/11. In Brooklyn,

In December 2008, the U.S. Army included this visit with the imam of the Islamic Center of El Paso, Texas, as part of cultural training for Fort Bliss Basic Officer Leader Course students.

The Arab American National Museum in Dearborn, Michigan, established in 2005, was the first of its kind anywhere in the world, and is an important resource for Arab-American studies.

New York, for instance, the Annual Arab American Heritage Park Festival presents Arab cuisine along with Arab-American music and activities. The academic world has also increasingly embraced Arab-American culture with more courses in Arabic language, history, politics, and literature.

On June 4, 2009, President Barack Obama delivered a speech in Cairo, Egypt, that addressed the relationship between the United States and the Arab world after 9/11. Obama drew on his experience living in Indonesia as a child, and on his Kenyan father's Muslim family tradition. In describing the place of Muslim Arab Americans in the United States, Obama was emphatic: "Let there be no doubt: Islam is a part of America."

However, in 2010, a proposed 13-story mosque and Islamic cultural center to be located two blocks from the site of the former World Trade Center stirred controversy. Critics of the proposed mosque believe it was inappropriate for Muslims to build a mosque so close to the site of the September 11, 2001 attack, yet many opponents accepted the legal right for religious groups to build places of worship at locations of their choosing. Supporters of the project saw it as a chance to improve interfaith relations.

ELIZABETH R. PURDY
INDEPENDENT SCHOLAR

Further Reading

Akram, Susan M. "The Aftermath of September 11, 2001: The Targeting of Arabs and Muslims in America." *Asian Studies Quarterly*, spring and summer 2002.

Becker, Paul. "Hate Crimes on the Rise against Arab-Americans." *State Government News,* Vol. 44, October 2001.

Brill, Steven. *After: How America Confronted the September 12 Era.* New York: Simon and Schuster, 2003.

Elkholy, Abdo A. *The Arab Moslems in the United States: Religion and Assimilation.* New Haven, CT: College and University Press, 1966.

Ginger, Ann Fagan. *Challenging United States Human Rights Violations since September 11.* Amherst, NY: Prometheus Books, 2005.

Gendercide.org. "Honour Killings and Blood Feuds." Available online, URL: www.gendercide.org/case_honour.html. Accessed August 2008.

Habbab, Delia. "Community Participation Launched at Arab American Festival." *Arab American News,* June 27, 2008. Available online, URL: www.arabamericannews.com/news. Accessed August 2008.

Haddad, Yvonne Yazbeek. *Not Quite American? The Shaping of Arab and Muslim Identity in the United States.* Waco, TX: Baylor University Press, 2004.

Hagopian, Elaine and Ann Padon, eds. *The Arab American: Studies in Assimilation.* Wilmette, IL: Medina University Press, 1968.

Hoogland, Eric, ed. *Crossing the Waters: Arab-Speaking Immigrants in the United States before 1940.* Washington, D.C.: Smithsonian, 1987.

The Internet Movie Database. "Tony Shalhoub." Available online, URL: www.imdb.com/name/nm0001724. Accessed August 2008.

McCloud, Aminah Beverly. *Transnational Muslims in American Society.* Gainesville, FL: University Press of Florida, 2006.

Nabhan, Gary Paul. *Arab American Landscape, Culture and Cuisine in Two Great Deserts.* Tucson, AZ: University of Arizona Press, 2008.

Neff, Alixa. *Becoming American: The Early Arab Immigrant Experience.* Carbondale, IL: Southern Illinois University Press, 1985.

Office of the High Commissioner for Human Rights. *Geneva Convention Relative to the Treatment of Prisoners of War.* Available Online. URL: www.unhchr.ch/html/menu3/b/91.htm. Accessed August 2008.

Pipes, Daniel. "The Muslims Are Coming! The Muslims Are Coming!" *National Review,* November 19, 1990.

Read, Jen'nan Ghazal. *Culture, Class and Work among Arab-American Women.* New York: LFB Scholarly Publishing, 2004.

Shaheen, Jack. *Reel Bad Arabs: How Hollywood Vilifies a People,* 2nd ed. New York: Olive Branch Press, 2009.

Suleiman, Michael W.. *Arabs in America: Building a New Future.* Philadelphia, PA: Temple University Press, 1999.

Alawi: A minority sect of Shia Islam notable for not accepting converts, historically found in the mountains of the eastern Mediterranean and central Syria. Alawites have come to a position of political and military prominence in modern-day Syria through the ascendancy of the Alawi Al-Assad family.

Amrika: America.

ayam: Days.

ba'ath: A resurrection or renaissance.

bayan: News, current events, or a statement of information.

bumin: Slang for a bum or one who chooses to avoid work at the expense of the community.

burghul: A crushed wheat dish that is partially boiled before fully cooked, and is used in soups and baked goods.

Copts: Native Egyptian Christians, an ancient sect dating back to the 1st century c.e., most of whom follow the Coptic orthodox rite. They currently make up between 10 to 20 percent of the population of Egypt.

daawah: (or dawah/da'wah) "calling to Islam," proselytizing or mission.

debka: Line dancing traditionally performed at weddings.

Druze: A heterodox Islamic sect with communities historically found in modern-day Lebanon, Syria, Israel/Palestine and Jordan. Its sacred texts, rites, and beliefs are kept secret and reflect Islamic, gnostic Christian and neoplatonic influences.

Eid al-Adha: An Islamic holiday commemorating the sacrifice of Ibrahim as told in the Quran; lasting three or more days, and involves family gatherings and meals of thanksgiving.

Eid al-Fitr: An Islamic feast holiday marking the end of the holy month of Ramadan.

Hadith: The speech of a person, or sayings originating from the prophet Muhammad. These prophetic sayings are collected in compilations of varying recognized authenticity to different schools of Islamic jurisprudence and sects.

hafla: A party, gathering or celebration.

halal: Permissible, or more specifically, actions that are allowed under the tenets of Islamic law (Sharia). Similar to the Yiddish word "kosher."

hara: A neighborhood.

hayah: (or *hayat*) Life.

hijab: A headscarf worn by female Muslims that covers the hair and neck.

ijmaa: The consensus of the Muslim community on a religious matter.

imam: A Muslim leader, typically of a mosque or community. For Sunni Muslims, an Imam leads the prayer though he has no official clerical status. For Shia Muslims, an imam is a revered source of religious guidance/leadership.

islah: Reform.

jazeera: An island.

jihad: A moral or physical struggle on behalf of God.

juhhal: Ignorant, those uninitiated into the mysteries of the Druze faith, as opposed to the wise ones or *uqqal*.

jumaa: The friday communal prayer performed at a mosque.

kaftan: A long traditional dress worn by Muslim women.

kibbie: (or kibbe/kibbeh) A dish made with a fried croquette that is stuffed with minced beef or lamb.

madrassa: School (literally, in Arabic); in Western and non-Arab contexts refers specifically to an Islamic religious school.

mahrajan: An outdoor religious or community festival involving the participation of numerous people.

mahjar: Abroad, as in "living abroad."

mezzeh: (or Mezze) A selection of appetizers or small dishes, a common feature of Levantine and eastern Mediterranean meals.

mjaddarra: A dish made with lentils and other vegetables such as wheat and rice. Sometimes referred to as a "poor man's dish."

mujahid: One who is engaged in *jihad*, a spiritual struggle or physical striving in the path of God.

mushir: An advisor, mentor, or military marshal.

Muslim: Literally in Arabic, "one who submits (to God)."

nakba: A catastrophe, a disaster of large proportions. In contemporary Arab discourse, "al-nakba" usually refers to the creation of the state of Israel and the expulsion and/or flight of Palestinians from their villages.

nisba: A suffix used to establish relation or nation of origin, such as the "i" ending in Kuwaiti, Iraqi, or Saudi.

niqab: A veil covering a woman's face, usually except for the eyes, worn in public and in the presence of male non-family members. It is considered obligatory by some conservative and tribal traditions of Islam for all adult females. Wearing the veil is commonly practiced in the Arabian peninsula countries, and in Pakistan and Afghanistan.

oud: A stringed instrument that is traditionally pear-shaped and features no frets; similar to a lute (from Arabic "Al-Oud") or mandolin.

qahwa: A flat sum of money paid in return for a loan, in keeping with the Islamic prohibition on usury.

qashsha: A case composed of wood or leather that peddlers would use to carry their sellable goods while they traveled from one area of potential business interest to another.

Ramadan: A holy month where Muslims traditionally fast every day from sunup to sundown, avoiding certain vices and other activities, and break the fast at nighttime family gatherings.

raqs baladi: A country dance, typically performed by attendees of a wedding or family reunion.

raqs sharqi: An oriental, theatrical dance, often featuring belly dancers.

sahra: An informal musical gathering or nighttime party.

sayeh: A traveler or tourist.

Sharia: Islamic law, as interpreted variously by the different schools of Sunni and Shia Islamic jurisprudence.

ta'ishin: Slang for slackers, or those who give in to the temptations of alcohol, drug use, or gambling.

umma: A community of Muslims, usually referring to the broader global Islamic community.

uqqal: Wise, those initiated into the mysteries of the Druze faith.

wakil al-mughtaribin: A moneylender or agent who facilitates emigration.

Index note: page references in *italics* indicate figures or graphs; page references in **bold** indicate main discussion.

PHOTO CREDITS. Department of Defense: 137. Federal Emergency Management Agency: 145, 155. iStockphoto.com: 8, 87, 114, 116, 117, 121, 130, 132, 136, 138, 149. Library of Congress: 3, 6, 7, 9, 11, 12, 15, 22, 23, 25, 26, 28, 31, 33, 34, 38, 39, 40, 41, 43, 45, 48, 55, 57, 63, 71, 75, 76, 93, 108, 110. © 2009 Rania Matar: 122, 134, 147, 148, 150. Photograph by Milton Rogovin © 1977–79 Courtesy The Rogovin Collection, LLC: 85, 86, 90, 101, 103, 105, 107. U.S. Customs and Border Patrol: 157. U.S. Air Force: 58. U.S. Army: 159, 160. Wayne State University: 99. Wikipedia: 73, 119, 135, 161.

Produced by Golson Media

President and Editor	J. Geoffrey Golson
Layout Editors	Oona Patrick, Mary Jo Scibetta
Author Manager	Susan Moskowitz
Consulting Editor	Tyler Golson
Copyeditor	Barbara Paris
Proofreader	Mary Le Rouge
Indexer	J S Editorial